MODERN HINDI POETRY

TRANSLATED BY

Leonard Nathan   James Mauch

Martin Halpern   H. M. Guy

Josephine Miles   W. M. Murray

Modern Hindi Poetry:
an anthology

EDITED BY VIDYA NIWAS MISRA

Indiana University Press / Bloomington

UNESCO COLLECTION OF CONTEMPORARY WORKS

This volume has been accepted in the series of translations of contemporary works jointly sponsored by the International PEN Club and the United Nations Educational, Scientific, and Cultural Organization (UNESCO).

to

Sri Maithili Sharan Gupta
Sri Balakrishna Sharma "Navin"
Sri Suryakant Tripathi "Nirala"
Sri Gajanan Madhav Muktibodh
Sri Nalin Vilochan Sharma

ACKNOWLEDGMENTS

THE EDITOR acknowledges his gratitude to Dorothee Finkelstein and John J. Gumperz, to whom goes the credit for the idea of the whole undertaking; and to the translators, Leonard Nathan, Martin Halpern, Josephine Miles, James Mauch, H. M. Guy, and W. M. Murray, for their patience and forbearance as well as interest in the task. The Editor is also indebted to Prabhakar Machwe, Paramanand Srivastava, and Kedarnath Agrawal for supplying much of the material; to Josephine Miles for support and encouragement in seeing the project through; to Sachchidananda Vatsyayan, William I. Oliver, and Krishna Kripalani for valuable comments and suggestions; and to Ellen M. Gumperz, Leonard Nathan, Robert R. Mount, and Gordon Roadarmel for help in arranging the material.

Some of these translations first appeared in *Beloit Poetry Journal, Mahfil*, and *Prairie Schooner*.

The successful completion of the project was made possible by assistance from the Rockefeller Foundation; the Center for South Asia Studies, Institute of International Studies at the University of California, Berkeley; and The Asian Literature Program of the Asia Society.

VIDYA NIWAS MISRA

CONTENTS

[7]

[9]

⋯§ PREFACE ⅋⋯

O_{ur} purpose in translating or adapting these poems from modern Hindi into English is to make new poems of them, poems we ourselves wish we might have written in English. When we have felt uneasy at a suddenly too familiar phrasing of an unfamiliar state of mind or too steady a metrical beat, we have abandoned them in favor of a phrasing or rhythm which seeemd sympathetic, though not identical, to the original.

Every Friday afternoon in the spring of 1961 we met with Professor Vidya Nivas Misra, first to read on the original blue pages the finely lettered poems which came to him from India, then to hear his reading and paraphrasing of them, then to spend a week trying to let the poems rewrite themselves, and finally at the next meeting to accept or reject a multitude of suggestions for their betterment. We came to await the poems from India as if we were awaiting new poems of our own.

The members of this group are poets who have published widely in American anthologies and magazines like *Evergreen Review, Hudson Review, Kenyon Review, Midland, The New Yorker, Poetry, Talisman,* and *Yale Review.* H. M. Guy, a graduate of the University of California, has worked in Berkeley. Martin Halpern and Josephine Miles teach in the Department of English and Leonard Nathan in the Department of Speech at the University of California at Berkeley. James Mauch is teaching at Foothill College in California and William Murray at the University of Iowa. Coming from birthplaces equally diverse—from Brooklyn, Chicago, Los Angeles, and Ireland—these poets met with Vidya Niwas Misra of India to draw one language into another in the belief that human perspectives could be drawn as well.

In the solving of our difficulties, we found the strongest instrument of language to be sentence structure. Simple reference, whether of image or of concept, we found to be inert if we took it at face value. When we relied on it to do the work of the poem, it guilelessly suggested either clichés of association which dulled us or mysteries of implication which were lost on us. Further, the trochaic lilt of Hindi carries its lines forward with a melody which sounds too insistent when pursued in English; yet the comparable English rhythms seem too lax for Hindi meaning. We could not rest, therefore, either in sound or in sense. But when we listened to the poem's progression, the sequences of its motion formed from beginning to end with its cycles and eddies of emphasis and return, and when we observed the resultant shape of the poem on the page, we were able to realize most clearly, by close attention to the process of word-order, repetition, and emphasis in the line, the powers latent in sound and word.

An example of our way of working may be taken from the translation of Vishvanath's "The Family":

> My father,
>   a conquered Everest,
> My mother,
>   an ocean of milk poisoned by poverty,
> My brother,
>   a lion cub cinched up as a pack animal,
> My sister,
>   a doll made out of soiled clothes,
> And I,
>   a kettle of water
>   steaming away to vapor,
>   water consumed into vapor.

Here is a structure of sound finely suited to English at the outset, a natural poem for us, so that the only problem is to preserve its strong parallels. Gradually we discarded *climbed* for *conquered, serpent* for *poisoned, beast of burden* for *pack animal, cloth* for *clothes,* and *boiling* for *steaming,* to bring the words into that close relation which is implicit in the original.

One reason we enjoyed the poems so much and why we trust that many readers will enjoy them also is that they know themselves and know each other. The poems, I mean; the poets may be a different matter. The poems neither throw their weight around out of uncertainty, guilt, or upset, nor withdraw into formalities of pride and ingenuity. They are aware of small nearby meanings consonant with large far-off meanings and they give these to us as directly as possible. Further, they speak forthrightly; they do not rant or murmur. They give the effect of having heard each other; that is, they fit easily into a group without the feeling of having been forced by tradition or convention; they make their conventions their own.

In the past, we may have yawned over work from India because it had the qualities of work from our own nineteenth century: a passive aestheticism, a languor, or a rich and special mythic reference beyond our comprehension. The gods of the *Bhagavadgita,* the generalized philosophy of Tagore, came to us through veils of distance. But since the 1930s, the Indian poets have turned to new materials, ones more familiar not only to them but to us, the materials of everyday human life, action, and feeling, the more universal as the more vividly particular. The word *economy* in its many meanings seems to me a good word for this poetic interest we share. Economy in the sense of housekeeping and of business, of daily domestic detail and its infinite associations. Economy in the sense of spareness, no luxury and waste, but telling minutiae in a telling structure. Economy in the sense of vitality, a great density of life in the implications and silences, yet effortless and not overloaded. Economy in the sense of multiplicity in brief space: a variety of points of view, and thus a play of humor, behind a single statement or choice of word.

Where do we find this urbanity in English poetry? Perhaps a little in Chaucer, in Skelton, in Swift, in Browning, in Emerson and Dickinson; and in some of the modern poets who have been aware of older Indian or Chinese traditions or of French Symbolists like Eluard and Char; or who, like Robert Frost, have written out of their own natural identity. Their poetry is not informed by particularly eastern or particularly western traditions but is, instead, drawn from universal themes—meeting, parting, choosing, regretting, protesting—which are the everyday concerns of people everywhere.

Both the individuality and the mutuality of these poems are important to us. We hope we have been able to learn and preserve these qualities in the process of translation.

JOSEPHINE MILES

◄§ I N T R O D U C T I O N §►

The presentation of poetry to a foreign reader is always a difficult and hazardous task. Some of the problems inherent in the process of translation are, of course, obvious; the difficulty of bridging preconceptions only slightly less so. But the effects of cultural differences can be deeper and far more insidious. Eastern cultures continue to have a different sense of time from that of the West, in spite of the leveling effects of modern technology: the result is a different relationship with life and experience. Differences in the genius of language govern expression; a literal rendering of a statement from one language to another may amount to a travesty but any other approach may demand both of the translator and the reader a degree of acquaintance with the original which would make translation unnecessary.

The chasm is widest and most forbidding where contemporary poetry is involved. A historical distance seems to permit the use of interpretive tools; but a contemporary poem has to stand alone, as an integral artistic creation, or be summarily dismissed.

Consider English in relation to any Indian language. The genius of English lies in understatement; all Indian languages, on the contrary, tend to elaborate. Almost any poem in English or an Indian language would come up against this problem: translation from English would seem halting and inadequate to the Indian; while that from the Indian language would be killed for the English reader by the excessive word. No Indian writer of English—seen from the wrong side of the gulf—has quite overcome this natural tendency to overstate; no English writer, on the other hand, has, in the judgment of the Indian reader, quite hit the mark. Significantly, *litotes* as a figure of speech hardly exists in any Indian language, its occasional appearance in modern social intercourse being regarded as no more than a facetious sophistication.

Yet this apparent prolixity in Indian languages is offset by a rigorous discipline on another plane: the profoundly significant use of *silence*. In the great Upanishadic debate [1] all the questions were asked and answered in public *except the crucial one*, for which the Sage took his questioner apart; when the two joined the company again the doubter had been convinced. A solitary instance from religious literature might be dismissed as an eso- teric device, but classical Indian literature abounds in instances of this kind. At key points in the action of Sanskrit drama, characters make the *gesture* of whispering but the utterance itself is completely silent; the rich possibilities of the unspoken word are used to the full.[2] Even in the folk song, the reminiscing woman can say: "He came, he held me in his arms, he loosened my girdle; but beyond this I remember nothing, for I was happy. . . ." ("When I am happy I am silent," echoes the proverb.)

This awareness of the value of silence—its value intrinsically as well as an artistic instrument—has persisted in contemporary Indian literature and especially in poetry. While acquaintance with Western (particularly English) literature might in some poets have tended to curb natural expression and encourage the virtue of understatement, in most cases the different virtues have been recognized as belonging to different sets of values. Indeed, the rebellious nineteenth-century poet Michael Madhu Sudan Dutt, steeped in English Romantic poetry and familiar with classical Greek and Latin as well as contemporary French and Italian poetry, found, of all things, the English use of the *caesura* his most valuable discovery. The fourteen-syllable *payár* metre he used for his Romantic epic, recasting the Ramayana

[1] The *Brhadāranyaka Upanishad*, III.ii.13.
[2] Shudraka's *The Clay Cart* provides excellent examples of this.

with the demons as heroes, traditionally had a fixed pause and an end rhyme, resulting in rather stilted narrative and monotonous verse. Dutt dispensed with the rhyme and adopted the variable sense-pause, thus immediately electrifying the metre. This was exciting enough, but his great achievement was in the use of the *silence* provided by the pause to add dramatic intensity to his narrative. Thus an insight acquired from reading a foreign literature was skillfully employed by an ingrained discipline to create a new work of art.

The contemporary Indian writer—and now I speak more specifically of the Hindi writer of poetry—would still regard silence as an effective means of expression; he would, if anything, be more purposeful in its use. Whether or not he would take seriously the definition of a net as "a concatenation of holes tied together with strings," he would appreciate the point of defining poetry as "a sequence of meaningful silences strung together with words." And it is perhaps here that one strikes the hard core of the problem of translation: the issue is not whether there can be a true *correspondence* of words but whether there can be a true *redaction* of silence—whether an Indian silence can be adequately rendered in terms of an Anglo-Saxon one.

To formulate the issue thus is not to suggest that the situation is a hopeless one. It is rather to indicate the desirability—indeed the necessity—of a shift of emphasis, to redefine the aim of translation. A true translation of poetry is the carrying over, not simply of words or word-meanings or even the "sense" of the original, but of the power that resides in the original, in its parts as well as in the whole. It is a trans-valence, or as the translators of this anthology have happily called it, a "trans-creation."

It may be just as well to add that the problem—and hence the solution—is not confined to the original author and the translator. As the original poem seeks a relationship with *its* readers, the translation does with its own: the parallel creation must have an equal valency to establish such a relationship with the parallel audience. In other words, the successful translator carries over and restates—recreates—amongst other things the original poem's problems also. In fact, in the context of communication, the translation *is* henceforth the original poem, and makes its own original demands on the reader.

An acquaintance with the traditional background and an understanding of the evolution of modern Indian poetry, from the ashes of literary conventions surviving in the miniature courts of scattered eighteenth-century princelings, would certainly help to lighten the difficulties in the way of communication. The classical Sanskrit tradition, in its decline having reached the point which the growing and virile Apabhramsha (tertiary Indo-Aryan) dialects were passing in their upsurge, was all but set aside; against the longer narrative the stanza-poem received a new lease on life. The Sanskrit poet of the dying courts had been using the tight form of the stanza-poem—limited to *one* couplet or a quatrain—only for the display of skill and virtuosity, relying on familiar *motifs* and traditional imagery. The Apabhramsha poet, in intimate contact with the life of the people and experiencing nature at first hand, brought to it a freshness of vision and a directness of expression that made it again a living thing. The regional eighteenth-century courts saw the second decline of the stanza-poem; virtuosity in the use of *motif* and a cyclopaedic memory for traditional imagery again taking the place of life-experience (except perhaps, for some poets, in the field of erotics!). But the thing to be observed and recorded is what survived through this double cycle of death and decay: the continuity, not merely of tradition in the sense of an accretion of dead weight, but of an attitude towards *the use of the unsaid:* the employment of silence to reinforce and to communicate meaning. The brief stanza-poem, in its degenerate period, was merely a slick evocation of a trite image, only the dexterity of the operation creating an illusion of newness; but at its best it achieved, through its very economy of expression, an intensity of vision that might well be the envy of any poet in any age. And the essence of this economy was the maximum exploitation of the unsaid. Sometimes the economy was primarily verbal—the economy of the unuttered *word*—the result was wit and the stanza-poem could justly be called an epigram; at other times it was a silent sharing of a premise of *experience* and what appeared before the eyes was an epiphany. The perfect stanza-poem was an arrested moment of an intense experience of life; a dramatic tableau. And the dramatic tableau, in this sense, was the precursor of the "image" of the Imagists.

Modern Hindi literature—modern Indian literature—begins in the nineteenth century. Inevitably, its rise and growth is interknit with the country's rise to nationhood and cannot intelligently be studied without reference to it. Such a study, even if limited to poetry, would entail the use of illustrative material far beyond the scope of the present anthology. But for an appreciation of the poems presented here it is fortunately not necessary to go so far afield. Illustration by analogy may also serve (despite the hazards of such a procedure) to explain the working of some important forces in contemporary Indian writing. Such analogies may be drawn from developments in another area altogether, but one likely to be much more familiar to the reader.

Soon after the turn of the century European poets, or to be more precise, English and French poets, became suddenly aware of a new Eastern tradition: that of Japan. The effect of this awareness on the French Symbolists and on the English Imagists was as significant as the awareness of the Indian (Sanskrit) tradition had been earlier for the European Romanticists, perhaps even more so because the effects of the Japanese contact were reflected in other arts besides poetry. Undoubtedly Japanese (and Chinese) painting had a part to play in creating this awareness; but it would be psychologically understandable, as well as historically correct, to relate it to the (for Europe) startling outcome of the Russo-Japanese war. It was the blunt fact of the victory of a "small" Asian power over a "great" European one that focused attention on the arts of Japan as well as on its military accomplishments. Without the warmth of this "healthy respect" for military prowess it is doubtful whether the artistic leaven would have worked as speedily or as well.

It was not on European nations only that this event had a profound effect: the effect on Asian nations was comparable—

psychologically at any rate—for there was not in their case a similar run on Japanese artistic resources. But then, at least so far as India was concerned, some of these were already part of the home tradition; for the rest, the difficulties of direct contact with Japan were circumvented by approaching her arts through the medium of the English language. The fact that the literary discovery of Japan was first made by India through, so to speak, European eyes, while the political discovery came through direct experience, was of some consequence in literary developments in India, even if primarily in a negative sense. Indian painters were turning to Chinese and Japanese painting even before the First World War; but (though Ezra Pound and T. E. Hulme were being read in the 'thirties and their debt to Japanese poetry noted) the Indian writer was not immediately taken with the *haiku*. He was turning, rather, to a reappraisal of its Indian analogue, the stanza-poem that had been so large and durable a part of Indian literary experience, and to more popular, equally effective if less sophisticated, forms which abounded in folk literature. Indeed it was not till a few years after the Second World War, after India's attainment of independence, that the Indian poet looked speculatively at the Japanese *haiku*, weighing its possibilities. This, now, was direct appraisal, with the mediacy of the English language but not of the English (or French) literary experience. The perspicacious reader will recognise the effects of experimentation along these lines in some of the poems included here.[3] As in the case of English poets— Symbolist and other—the effects may be far from direct; the experimentation may be a stage, of short or longer duration, in which the poet perfects his craft, ceasing to be important when he has found his true direction.

It is to be hoped that such a reader will go on to the felicitous discovery that, though the post-World War II Indian poet in his search for *visual clarity* may have been stimulated by the Japanese *haiku* as well as by English poets drinking at the same fountain, his main inspiration was Indian; furthermore, that his quest for *dramatic intensity* led him ever and again back to the

[3] See, for example, Shamsher Bahadur Singh's *Morning*.

indigenous source. This could perhaps be anticipated, for there is an inherent difference of approach in the two traditions. The Japanese-Chinese approach is eminently *pictorial* while the Indian one is *emotional*; in one case the basic art is painting, in the other it is drama. The one achieves visual focus by a creative omission of detail, the other finds dramatic focus through the creative use of silence.

The quantity of Indian literature available in English translation is pitifully small; but even in what is available there is a conspicuous dearth of translations of the stanza-poem. Undoubtedly this is in great measure due to the jewel-like hardness of the poem, its taut structure, and most of all to the compression it achieved through the use of the unsaid: its quality of eloquent silence to which I have already referred. The Chinese or Japanese short poem rarely achieved such compression; yet it could pose problems even for the translator of genius, as evidenced by Ezra Pound's rendering of *The Jewel Stairs' Grievance* where the poem calls for an explanatory note longer than the poem itself, in spite of the fact that the title also has provided a key by making it clear that the poem has something to do with a grievance—a fact that is not obvious from the poem itself. ("The poem is especially prized because she utters no direct reproach," explains the note.) Hindi poetry, even that of the late eighteenth century which is regarded as the lowest ebb of the creative tide, could provide such examples by the hundred; that no translations are available is oblique evidence of an "embarrassment of riches." Under such circumstances, it is difficult in English to illustrate how the contemporary Hindi poet, spurred sometimes by the Western poet's employment of an Eastern motif, symbol, or image, or of an Eastern artifice, turns to his own tradition and renews it. The most useful substitute would appear to be a sort of glossary of the conventions still employed by the Hindi poet, a brief explanation of his use of symbols and of traditional imagery, especially when employed for compression of meaning.

As preface to such an attempt, it is perhaps desirable to discuss briefly the concept of the poetic symbol in Hindi literature. A symbol is not a substitute; it is not just a "throwing together" of two or more levels of meaning, either. Not simultaneous *existence* only, but simultaneous *visibility* (of several levels of meaning) also, is required for the genuine poetic symbol: it must have identity (*sārūpya*) as well as con-visibility (*sādṛśya*). One could pursue the matter to its metaphysical fundamentals, and it is perhaps true that symbolism can be of value only to the extent to which it is firmly rooted in metaphysic. Ezra Pound, when he defined symbolism as "permanent metaphor," was fully aware of this; he recognized that belief in permanent metaphor posited belief in a "permanent world"—that is, an ideal world, beyond or within the world of appearance, which is the basis for all true symbolism. "What is beyond the sight, the gods find pleasing," said the Brahmana. "The manifest is distasteful to them." [4]

But without elaborating on Indian metaphysical concepts it may here suffice to record that many of the symbols have their origin in a tacit acceptance of the principle of non-dualism: in a recognition of the relationship of identity between the internal and the external world. Life is a continuum: the image of the flowing stream, or the sea, follows naturally from this concept. The individual life may be the lotus bud rocking gently above the water—emphasizing discreteness; or it may be the drop in the sea—emphasizing identity. Or again it may be the drop on the lotus leaf floating on the water—a two-tier image. As the family line represents "continuity in identity" in the *temporal* sense, the image of the tree provides a *spatial* symbol (e.g., "family tree"). The same basic idea is expressed on another level in the theme of the perpetual return—a pair of royal swans flying back to the Himalayas, their eternal abode. In this non-dual world there is no death, only becoming; time moves in cycles and is perpetually recreated. Thus we have the symbolism of the cycle of the seasons, the vegetative cycle from seed to flower and fruit and thence back again to seed and sprout, and other elaborations of the same idea.

[4] The *Śatapatha Brāhmana*, 14.6.11.2.

The reference of the symbol always to an ideal world should underline a distinction which in any case should be obvious: the distinction between the image and the image as symbol. The dramatic tableau presented by the older stanza-poem presented an integral image *as image,* though the poet *used* the traditional symbols or conventions to achieve compression. The contemporary Hindi poet does not necessarily limit himself either to the image or the traditional symbol—a natural consequence of the fact that he does not necessarily limit himself any longer to the traditional non-dualist concept of being. There have been those Indian poets whose basic *credo* would approximate fairly closely the Imagist's (e.g., Pound's A *Few Don'ts by an Imagiste*), but others would question the adequacy of the definition of an Image as "that which presents an intellectual and emotional complex in an instant of time." For how else do we define an instant of time except as "that in which an intellectual and emotional complex is presented?"

Some of the conventions and traditional symbols frequently used by the contemporary Hindi poet and illustrated in the present anthology are listed below. In all these symbols, based on a parallelism with nature, something more than mere pathetic fallacy is involved: they stem from a sense of continuity with non-human nature, of the cyclicity of all manifestations.

1. The lotus blooming at sunrise represents both beauty and truth, harmony and purpose. Other flowers which bloom at the touch, embrace, or kiss of a human beauty (e.g., the *aśoka*) symbolize the fertility of beauty.

2. Specific symbols are associated with each season: the cuckoo and mango blossom with spring; the peacock with the rains; swans and the *khanjan* (wagtail), both migratory birds, with the early autumn; mists and falling leaves with the winter.

3. The *chātaka,* or *papīhā* (a bird of the cuckoo family), is the symbol of unswerving devotion and yearning for divine love. Autumn rain (rain falling under the star *Svāti* or Arcturus) symbolizes God's grace which produces poison in the snake, a pearl in the oyster, medicine in the bamboo; the

[23]

chātaka disdains all other drink but *Svāti* rain which alone can quench his thirst. So is the thirsty soul unassuaged till it finds divine grace.

4. Kama, the god of love, having been burnt to ashes by Siva, the "Auspicious," is forever the bodiless one: this conveys the idea that carnal desire, without deep roots in the soul, is futile; love must be rooted in an intense yearning for a union of souls. Kama's spouse is Rati (attachment), and his companions are the Spring, the Moon, and the *chātaka* bird.

5. The elephant is a symbol of grace in movement, of meekness in strength, of poise and massiveness; the lion symbolizes majesty, vigor (both of mind and body), and alertness; the deer agility, delicacy, sensuous fraility.

6. The human face may be compared to the moon; eyes to a fish or a wagtail, to a blue lotus or a slice of the mango fruit, or they may be compared to the eyes of a gazelle. A tress of hair is a snake, a cloud, night; the lips are the *bimbā* (passiflore) fruit, new shoots of the mango tree, coral; the teeth are a string of pearls or white *kunda* buds. The ample bosom is a symbol of fruitful womanhood; the slender waist is compared to that of a lion; the thighs are trunks of the plantain tree or an elephant's trunk. Hands and feet are again lotuses, sharing with the eyes a pre-eminent position as the vehicles of expression in Indian dance, drama, and poetry. These conventional comparisons may sometimes appear trite to a modern reader; the important thing is not the simile itself but the ideal beauty which is symbolized—"the beauty of the world beyond the world of appearances."

7. Conventional auspicious signs and omens include: a full pitcher, a bird flying, a cow feeding her calf, green grass, betel leaves, a conch, sandalwood paste, a mirror, a mother with a child, an oncoming breeze, a mark made with turmeric. There are numerous others. The kernel is an emphasis on continuity, on the perpetual renewal of life, a facing forward in hope.

The contemporary Hindi poet has used these symbols and conventions for reasons of economy as well as, frequently, an identity of beliefs about the nature of the ideal world. To those deriving from classical or literary sources he has added many of humbler origin—regional dialects and folklore. But he has not limited himself to a conventional repertoire of imagery. Even a quick reading of the poems will provide evidence of his two-fold innovation: the familiar idea presented with fresh vividness through a new image, sometimes compressing an additional layer of meaning; or a fresh image charged with a new set of assumptions about the ideal world. "A doll made/ Out of soiled clothes," "A kettle of water steaming away to vapor," "A palm's width of shade on the sand beneath a shrub"—the image invoked is new and different, the basic idea a familiar one. But poems like Kesari Kumar's *Evening* ("Evening/ Is, well/ The yawn of a rude guest"), or Nalin Vilochan Sharma's *Evening At The Seashore* ("Like cats, the sand dunes doze;/ Waves scurry from their paws"), or Kirti Chaudhari's *Inertia* ("Noon, then, grows tidal and its idiot brightness/ Boils over") to name only a few picked at random, present images for which the tradition has not prepared us, and which seek to present truths of experience unique in the sense in which the individual is unique. Equally fresh are many "pure" images—images which do not stand for any meaning other than themselves: they arrest by their intensity of vision rather than by any economy achieved through the use of conventions.

There are no perfect anthologies. An exhaustive one may be at fault on account of its very comprehensiveness: it may distort the view. Those of shorter compass go through agonies of selection without any certainty that their choice will be fully endorsed. But for the present anthology, it seems that the editor and his translator-collaborators were able to achieve near-perfect conditions. Vidya Niwas Misra, rooted in the classical Sanskrit tradition, and a conscientious reader of Hindi poetry, has spent years at the twofold task of testing the new against the old and making elbow-room for the new hemmed in by the old. The translators are all poets in their own right, almost all teachers of poetry as well; one would expect that they would be naturally sensitive to the problems involved and the pitfalls to be avoided, that they would have the gift of matching phrase with phrase and reticence with reticence. In other words they would be the ones most capable of achieving the trans-valency to which I have referred above. The poems have been judiciously selected by the editor, providing a fair range of themes and moods, a fair variety of forms and rhythms; epic and narrative forms have not been included, nor poems excessively steeped in local color or allusion or relying solely on verbal music or wit. The period was limited to about a generation—1945–61—exception being made only in the case of a few poems that might be regarded as the precursors of the new era, like, for example, *The Symphony of Clouds*.

The sequence of the poems is a sequence of ideas and moods like that in many of the individual poems; an order, an atmosphere, a world, into which the reader is welcomed.

The procedure adopted for translation may be of interest too. The poet-translators were given line-by-line English renderings of the Hindi poems, together with a paraphrase where needed, background notes and explanation of symbols, notes on the metre and rhyme scheme. This material was supported with a tape recording of the poem, which was always either the poet's own reading or a close approximation thereof. The translations, or "trans-creations," were then revised by both the editor and the group of translators, the former checking them against the originals and the latter considering them as parallel poems. Their comments and suggestions were then mulled over by the translator, in due course resulting in a revised version which, though a closer translation, still stood as a poem in its own right.

The translations presented here may not be suited for comparative reading by a student of *language*; had they been such they would probably have been hard to recognize as poetry. The collaborators, presenting *literature*, aimed to produce a poem for a poem. This has been in great measure achieved; the translation offered *is* a poem, and it is very close to the original—in the only sense in which one poem can be close to another poem. As one who has spent years translating and interpreting poetry, as well as one who has the honor of being included in this anthology, I can vouch for its authenticity, if such *ex gratia* endorsement may be excused.

I can only conclude with the hope that the anthology will succeed in its purpose, provide enjoyment to its readers, and create an enduring interest in the contemporary literature of India; and that it will be the forerunner of many such attempts.

SACHCHIDANANDA H. VATSYAYAN

MODERN HINDI POETRY

Kedarnath Singh

This much we must demand:
A horizon west of any place we are,
Our scope of splendor anytime to see, all ours.

And if we stretch a hand,
Chance that a door will open out
The way we want to go;
And when we turn,
Uncalled for, unpremeditated,
From the desk ahead,
Or from these papers towering on either hand,
             to peer in light for wonder,
Chance that the one response we lack
Will blossom our surprise—
This much we must demand.

This much we must demand:
When we are laboring lost in distant thought,
Sudden doves to flutter from our gloom.

O this we must demand:
The self's dim edge to resonate with song
That strikes us, bass and treble, always whole;
And shadows to offer up in strange projections
Angles of vision, never dreamed, in air;
And the merest possibility of,
After much thoughtless straining of both hands,
Some word, both warm and wise, for one another,
Some simple play to put ourselves together,
Some room enough to be in—

This much we must demand.

                             L. E. NATHAN

Raghuvir Sahae

ACQUAINTANCE WITH THE SUN

I notice plants placed under the long window,
Their leaning toward the sun.
The sparrow has begun collecting straw
In the cornice, this year as in every year;
The plants and window are not the same,
Nor are the sparrow and the cornice—
All differ from those of another year.

How real are these roses about to bloom, to flower, to fall?
The hazard of falling charges the form of these roses,
Resplendent in their risk.

The plants lean out, as if tugged by the sun,
Announcing the sunlight even to the veranda.
The veranda declares its awareness of the sunlight.

The sparrow flutters after another straw;
A soft breeze brings suddenly the fragrance of budding roses,
Of coming summer.

How real is my acquaintance with the sun?

Many stories tell, tell about the sparrow's nest,
A tale for every year:
Each year's nest has its singular fragrance;
Rather a sunlight,
Rather a memory,
Rather a warmth,
Rather an attendance.

A soft breeze and a huge sky.
A sky blue without haze or clouds.
A soft breeze and light.

The light which I apprehend as singularly mine,
The light which suffuses the huge, blue, external sky,
The light in the veranda, a soft breeze and spring.

J . M A U C H

Maithili Sharan Gupta

QUATRAINS

I

When calling You, Unknowable—abashed,
    knowledge was stilled and beaten; then
How subtly, Lord, Your meditation flashed:
    one smile before it entered in.

II

May those who scrounge for sources, endlessly
    founder from shore to shore and always miss.
Who cares, and why not tread the tidal sea
    where just ahead there jets a flood of bliss?

III

Come hither, my memory, come hither,
    thought of those thorny days that prick me still.
I'll keep you green by watering, until
    you give me flowers that will not wither.

IV

When you call, "God, my God!" you dunce,
    Who is the servant, who the Lord?
You pester Him with your pretense;
    Go yourself, yourself your word.

[33]

V

Tell me, Lord—both in delight and grief,
  my life's breath nags me for an answer:
When shall we finally have relief
  from this dark self we suffer?

L. E. NATHAN

Nirala [Suryakant Tripathi]

TO A WATERFALL

Oh bright, boisterous little stream,
Why, from those placid hills of your origin,
Do you frisk your way down through that sunless forest
You alone illumine? What is the sense,
Wise child or childlike sage, of all this desire
For descent out of light into darkness? Ah,
When the stone trips you up, as though to recall
You to those hills you began from, you pause,
Acknowledging its good intent and its
Absurdity. Then, gesturing lightly
Up at the Unconceived, on you plummet;
And the stone's heart knows and abides in the music
  you make.

M. HALPERN

Sumitra Nandan Pant

FRUITS OF THE EARTH

Childhood. I planted pennies in the yard and dreamed
Penny trees would grow. I heard the air sweet
With the silvery ringing of my clustered crop
And strutted round like a big fat millionaire.
Ah fantasy! Not a single sprout came up;
Not one tree appeared on that barren ground:
Swallowed in dusk, blighted my dreams.
On hands and knees I scratched for a sign of growth;
Stared into darkness. What a fool I was!
I gathered the fruit I had sown. I had watered coin.

Fifty years have passed. And passed like a gust of wind.
Seasons came; I hardly noticed them:
Summers blazed, swinging rains poured,
Autumn smiled, following winter shivered,
Trees stood naked; later, the forest, green.
Again in the sky, dark salve-like clouds
Thick with healing elements. It rained.
Out of simple curiosity, I ventured out
To the courtyard corner, and bending down,
Pressed rows of beds into soaked sod
And planted bean seeds. Then covered them.
The hem of the earth's sari was tied with jewels.

Soon I forgot this simple incident—
No one could think it worth remembering.
A few days later walking at evening, in the yard,

[3 5]

Suddenly before me, there they were,
A multitude of new arrivals, standing
Each with a tiny green umbrella on its head.
They seemed like young birds who had just cracked their
    shells,
Already fully fledged, trying the sky.
Wide-eyed I stared and stared, hypnotized—
This miniature army, dwarfs arrayed in rows
Just sprung from seeds I'd sown not yesterday,
Erect and proud, shook their feet as if to march.

I've spent days, now, watching them grow.
Gradually the space around puts on light leaves
Then thickens to canopies of velvet green;
The tendrils rise winding and swinging on the frame
And spray out, fountains of fresh springs.

A stunning sight—the growth of a generation:
Starlike sprays of flowers scattered yet grafted
To the dark green undulating branches:
White foam on waves; a luminous new moon sky:
Pearls in hair: a flower-patterned blouse.

At harvest time, millions of pods came forth;
Some were stringy and some were fat; all sweet:
Long fingers, swords, or emerald necklaces.
It will not seem that I exaggerate
If I say they developed like the moon,
Or an evening sky growing into clusters of stars.

All winter we ate them cooked for lunch and dinner.
Next door neighbors, close friends, mere acquaintances,
Relatives, people we hardly knew,
Some who didn't even ask, all shared
The bountiful supply the earth produced.

[36]

She yields abundantly to her dear children;
I had not understood in planting pennies
The laws of her love. She bestows gems.
Storehouse of virtue and all-embracing love,
She serves on terms of truest equality;
Seeds of her own kind only will she bear.
Then, even her dust may yield crops of gold
And directions bursting with joy of her works.

W. M. MURRAY

Kedar Nath Agrawal

BLUE BIRD RIVER

Dipping its beak into the vein of water,
The bird drinks in the deep pulse of the river,
Then, lifts a drop like pearl to the air,
And, though so small, takes great pride to show
His blue feathers in flight. I too fly there,
Who take to heart, like him, this sweet blue flow.

L. E. NATHAN

Shamsher Bahadur Singh

SUDDEN LAUGHTER

By a cut-off path and sombre waterfall
The sky defined by a fuzzy draggle of clouds,
. . . here, that dark young girl
Has suddenly relieved the air with laughter.

L. E. NATHAN

Kirti Chaudhari

A star quivered in a corner of the sky.
I thought, yes
Everything sometime or other will shine out like this.

A pebble stirred
The water of the drowsy waves.
I knew
At least for once inertia will be shaken.

Blossoms flowered
In the deeps of forests,
Their fragrance spoke out, yes
Once at least I scatter and bestow.

What more to ask
Than images of my aspiration—
But belief nods no
A dream is better,
What can an image do but shine or scatter,
What will it offer?

J. MILES

Ravindra Bhramar

MY SUCCESSOR WILL BE HERE

I know
I, also, shall journey
Over this track,
My feet re-echo
From this uninhabited earth
And in it crumble.

I know
This track will vanish,
The calloused wind
Will wipe
My footprints off the dust.

My address, and name,
The trees (rigid sentries
Erect to right and left)
Hold
In the merest leaf.

He, my successor, will be here
Before autumn appears,
I know.

W. M. MURRAY

Paramanand Srivastava

This tree has ten leaves
Another possesses twelve
A third, twenty.
There are so many things to do in leisure
So many things to think in leisure.
An orange banner waves at the edge of one leaf
Pride lies crushed, enclosed within another
As in a closed fist,
And on the forehead of the third is the inevitable sun.

H . M . G U Y

Kirti Chaudhari

I N E R T I A

The sunlight that pulls itself over the roof-tops
                              looks vacant,
And the vagrant shades of its radiance
Fall weakly on grasses,
On flowers, on grottoes, all looking vacant.

Noon, then, grows tidal and its idiot brightness
Boils over, but still it looks vacant;
Then, shadow by shadow, lightness collapses—
Yet comes back to do

The selfsame labor again, compulsion of one
                        whose look is vacant.

I swear as usual to start
Making use of my days
Tomorrow—
And tomorrow,
O tomorrow, what change will amaze,
But
The day is always now and is vacant.

L. E. NATHAN

Dharmavir Bharati

CLOUD IN THE CANYON

There was no foretelling when this winged whale would
    slyly lift
From its nest of dark and slide its miles of smoky,
High-backed bulk to the far edge of the canyon,
Poising there on a gristled spread of wings
That shadowed the virgin canyon. She wore the morning
    light
For innocence,
But as she woke,
Still drowsy, she took the gray
Imponderable weight driven upon her
By a cloudy passion until,
Overmastered, she sank away,

And her vague lover, squandered,
His cheek resting upon the naked
And dark western peaks,
Deepened heavily into sleep.

With exquisite slowness,
The canyon recovered her breath,
Now heavy with sweetness, heady with the drench of rich
    rain,
Delicate sprays of wind
Loosening the scent of pine and cedar—
While, waking, the cloud stretching over, spread
A smoky yawn of wings by hundreds,
Fluttering,
And beating on the high rocks ahead;
A great hoverer,
The cloud rocked,
Nosed through gorges,
Wandered passes,
Then slowly heaved itself over high-shouldered slopes,
    puffing like any exhausted climber.

An instant ago, there was the canyon:
Striped with sunlight,
Parquetry of green fields,
Roofed in red tiles of little hill towns,
And now, nothing, nothing,
All wiped out
In the momentous conjuring
Of an all-blotting cloud.

Nothing but smoky mass now real,
Milky amplitude, like sea swarming the rocks,
Grenading foam
Until red-tiled village,
Squares of green field,
Light-streaked canyon floor
Seem coral, fish, shell, seaweed,
Heaved, by shifting tide, to the surface
To float there awhile and then sink down again.

Now fog and ashes snow the world under,
And haze blanches the sky;
Hung between, unfounded, a whole peak
Trapped in middle air,
Defying its own weight
By cloudy conjuring.

Silent on those calm slopes,
The spruce trees,
Their sparse needles thrust out
Like shocked eyes whitened
By wonder.

Again the cloud climbs, like an unwieldy animal,
Its hind feet crushing the thickets—
Trunks, branches, leaves
Paling with that weight and, as if sinking under,
Fading into grayness like scrawls
Rubbed down to utter blankness.

Washed away,
Like the most delicate watercolor,
Imperious peaks of stone ranges; now a great absence
For canyon, village, field, trees, streams, creation itself,
Dissolving to their elemental gray,
Becomes one with this all-smothering cumulus.

I, only, stand
In this pale obscurity which whirls its dissolution around
    me
And in which everything has come to nothing:
My house, my village,
Footpath that lifted me here,
Forest that I haunt day after day,
Streams, tender to my dusty feet,
Come to nothing, all—

I, only, and nullity
Thickened to crazy whiteness where I stand.

Worn down to a revelation
At this unbelievable height,
Suddenly I am clear,
As a man I am a clear
But
Diminished figure, having ascended this unbearable peak.

Dwarfed now, what can I take
But two, just two, strides ahead,
Two behind,
Two strides down,
Two up?
All that I know whirls two strides off at every side;
One more step mistaken
And the canyon swallows what I am.

Striken by this nothing,
I reached for familiar things:
This is a shoulder of stone, this the tree's rooted hip;
But what is this?
What respondingly warm hand
In mine?

"I, dwarfed like you,
Have shunned the usual footpath,
Have moved beside you to this height.

O take heart;
I am no taller than you,
Though I am gifted with one stride more
Than your fear will admit;
Step off your little two,
And I will, given your faith,
Step off the third.

Though it is small, I have chosen
The shape of man for being,
So be faithful to our form,
Remembering that when Vishnu shrank to such bodily
  slightness,
He took a step that had no visible end."

At this moment, the milky fog
Thinned a little,
And suddenly the soundless vacancy gaped,
And, though still unseen,
Pines sent their presence up,
Sense borne by uplifting wind;
Birds, huddled in bushes,
Called at me in shaken song,
And, beyond, a hill resounded with their song.

Then I felt more than this little self of fear;
Presences, adrift in the same blind journey
Through this gorge,
Invisible,
Moved again on their paths,
Unfrightened in their advance.

Though sun is still hidden,
Its haze-blurred light between peaks
Flashes like a supernatural gleam;
Rivers now vein the land below with their shine;
And, through the milky glass of air,
Spruces glitter like arched steel;
And slowly mist, layer by layer, crumbles
Here, then there;
Sun like heated gold
Showers down
Bringing to blossom whole villages.

[45]

The cloud vanishes as it appeared,
Leaving tufts behind,
One at rest in the thicket's shadow
Like a white cow,
And one solitary, gracile wisp
Grazes the slope like a deer
Shaped from a dream of silver.

L . E . N A T H A N

Kedarnath Singh

A NAME FOR MY LITTLE DAUGHTER

Sunlight. It clings
To you, that name, like a butterfly's wings
To the quivering dew-wet twig of a rose bush;
A naive name—
> It comes in a quick spontaneous rush
> To lips long jaded, where it clings—
> Your right and only name.

Oh there are other names,
And I can never quite say why,
Watching you at your secret games
Amid the quivering bushes and plants that rise
High as your shoulders and no higher,
Why my heart echoes that right and only name.

> Ah how can you comprehend
> What chasm stretches between
> Your silent smiling and
> These echoing words of mine?

> Yet I have seen
> At the bottom of that questioning smile

Mile after mile
Of pathway that will wind
About that chasm; seen
The dead ends and the blind
Or broken turnings, the many
Still unbuilt bridges spanning
The spaces of the mind,
Which I must cross for what small sense
I'll ever make of the multiple questions
  begging behind
This small existence.

Yes I am sad; but why
Are *you* sad, child? What makes you cling
Now like a frightened butterfly,
Silent and hushed against my sunless shoulders?
I have done nothing

But give you a name, a small, soft name
Befitting what you are this moment.

Ah yes, you know
Now what you cannot comprehend—
How all my days must now be spent
Finding a fitter name for you—
            More permanent,
            And making more sense
            Of this small existence—
            Yet yours, and only you.

                    M . HALPERN

Sarveshwar Dayal Saksena

A WAKING SONG FOR MY DAUGHTER

I

These jingling toys—the trees—begin to ring,
The sun is that red ball just rolling over,
Wake up, my daughter,
It is morning now.

The small balloons that you sent up—the stars—
Have disappeared,
Who knows how far they have ascended.
The top you threw and spun—the moon—
See it just there, is on the edge of any-moment-tumbling
      down.
Wake up, my daughter,
For it is morning.

II

Those dolls which you had lulled to sleep—
The cliffs yonder—sit up bright faced, rubbing their palms,
The fat doll's embroidered bonnet—
—the little pond—is upside-down.

Look, it flies off on its own,
The shimmering sari of your darling doll—the river;
Wake up, my daughter,
It is morning now.

Your playmate, cooling breeze, who went to bed with you, O
tired so early,

Is back refreshed by dipping in some spring
And touches with wet hands your picture book.
See, it is all a mess of many colors.

Get up; the bells of the old man—the sky—fade in the
    distance,
He seems to be turning up some other street,
But still the rainbow of balloons tied on his stick,
Golden and silver paperwheels, goggles of red and green
Pretty cardboard pipes for blowing, are still to be seen far off.
Wake up, my daughter, let me hear your voice.
Look at the monkey, hunched on roof's edge with your box
    of cookies.
Wake up, the sun has come.

Look how this rubber bird
Sings when you pinch his belly,
How the rabbit leaps.
Does one weep because of sun?
The sun is a flood of milk;
Get up and fill your bowl;
Your uncle, the moon also gets his share.

Beyond beyond, quite near Heaven,
There happens to be a cow
Whom nobody sees,
And that cow belongs to your father,
To every father who has a hungry child;
Now, don't you cry
Or that cow will run away
And when a father goes off to find it,
He doesn't come back.

L. E. NATHAN

Srikant Joshi

Fill up the hollowed earth,
Shovelled out by old wear
And argue down this truth
(Yes, truth and most bare):
That we are famished and stagger,
Patched and empty as beggars,
Sorrow our bed, mere breath our water.

Say with elation:
We are actually glad.
Ask with determination:
Are we sad?
Not us, not a bit distressed,
Not even a trifle depressed.

Offer your friends conversation
With tea and cake, hear them hello
While you stand on debts and doubts,
A firm floor of pin-points,
And return their felicitation.

Shine at your station,
Light the dark hallway within,
Start a fire, make your door an illumination.

It's true, as we know,
Our feet ache so

We limp to the ditch ahead
That brings our minds low.

But this is a day for pleasure;
Steady on your feet; hesitation
Might expose a vulgar privation.
Shyness won't get you compassion;
After all, it's a very big day:
Come out from behind that affliction.

L. E. NATHAN

Kedar Nath Agrawal

SPRING WIND

Allow me; I'm the wind.
Spring wind; that's my name.

I am the very one
Who has toyed with the sky
For centuries, and did it
Effortlessly.

I am the one, yes I,
Who whistled harmony
To the sweet air
Of earth's first day.

I am the very one
Who drops the biting wine
(Spelled "Love") on every tongue
To keep all creatures young.

My holy books
Are good looks,
The facts of love,
And the red leaves of the heart.
Listen to me—
A lunatic
Of autonomy;
Therefore no need, no want—
I wander where I wander,
Light-headed traveller
Toward no house,
No purposes,
No fantasies,
Not one hope,
No friends or enemies;
I'm where and what I please.

Whom I have just left
And where I go,
City, town,
Crowds,
Vacancy,
Ripe fields, whole lands,
I make them whirl,
I make them clap their hands.

Climbed the Mahua Tree
Spun its pearl head,
Jumped down thud,
Then climbed the Mango Tree
And shook it fanatically,
Whispered "Boo" in its ear,
And slid down and away.

Reached a field of green wheat:
O how long is the hour

In which my time was delight
Flying in circles there?

Linseed I saw, on its head
A pitcher of blue, and I shook
To knock that pitcher down
But had no luck,
So made the mustard dance.

I forgot my own name
In the middle of this play;
But Lady Spring grew big
Blossoming for me.

A shy Arahar plant turned
Her back on my good works.
She was cold, but I burned
And so I pushed her at
An innocent passerby
And knocked the lady flat.

And that's why I laughed, you see,
And the four directions roared,
And the fields, splitting, shook,
And the sun whooped, and all
Creation crowed with me.

                    L . E . NATHAN

Trilochan Shastri

COME CLOSER

Come closer, come closer still.
Do not tell me your troubled story.
Make no response, only keep quiet,
Your quiet breath will let me know.

J. MILES

Kedarnath Singh

LATE SPRING NOON

Dejection feeds on the Neem tree's leaves dropping
    straight down
  On fields whose mustard yellow is faded
  To ash gray. Threads of memory,
  Separate and nondescript as the sun,
  Cling to the mind's loom, wait to be woven.
But in this standstill hour, the loom remains unstirred.
  Bare Shisham trees, newly deprived,
  Stand gaping at the breathless heaven;
  The Chilbil's naked arms reach out
  In a weird posture of estrangement.
Only the Bamboo grove's dry rustle rasps on the ear.
  Spent noon on the fallen leaves lies prone.
  Those winds which quickened the four directions
  Have drawn up, as in terror. All
  That shines in those grayed-out eyes is their hardness.
O love, where has the cold night gone, why is it day?

M. HALPERN

Nalin Vilochan Sharma

EVENING AT THE SEASHORE

Like cats, the sand dunes doze;
Waves scurry from their paws.
Clouds graze on sun's gold crop,
As confident as sheep.

A dot upon the sand,
Myself I cannot find;
For time has angled me
With boundless sky, land, and sea.

My only traces are
Thin smoke puffs in the air
And prints marking my way
That waves will snatch for play.

J . MAUCH

Kedar Nath Agrawal

THE SEA

An immense azure bird
Has stretched its wings,
Yet, helpless, cannot fly;
It is so far up to the sheen of the sky.

[55]

An immense azure eye
Has opened its lid,
Yet, helpless, cannot close;
And for this it overflows.

L . E . NATHAN

Agyeya [*Sachchidananda Vatsyayan*]

ABOUT RETURNING

i. Green Hill

The slope of this hill, its curve, its cover of pine trees;
A circling trail uplifting like aspiration;
   A river at my feet, taut as a streak of pain;
Birds in their nests at peace.
All these I saw as fully as I could have seen.

To comfort myself, I said: O, I will return,
   Even if only later—ages later.
The horizon lit up with a sudden lightning
Like a distant eye, its brightness asking:
   How long, traveller, will you remember?

ii. Sunset

Sun's light
Glowed on
The opposite range crested with young pines
—a mother's smile mirrored in her child's face.

Song:

Awareness beyond all pain
And full of accepting unarguable delight,
Said—
There will be no return, none.

L. E. NATHAN

Thakur Prasad Singh

CIRCUIT THROUGH THE HILLS

The traveling is over, dear,
Over with the season of the fair.

Yes, all the older girls were married,
And all the younger, too, were married.
Each found an answer to her prayer;
Each wore the flowers in her hair;
But fairs have ended for the year.

O my mad daughter, you are harried,
And we've tried everywhere.
The answers never varied.
Your days go by, tear by tear,
But fairs have ended for the year.

J. MAUCH

Nirala [Suryakant Tripathi]

THE SYMPHONY OF CLOUDS

1

With swinging rustle or thundering cry,
With your deathless music fill the sky!
  Bursting over deserts, houses, trees,
  Swell all waterfalls, rivers, lakes, and seas;
  Challenge the wind with your lightning's surprise,
  Startle the forests, startle our ears and eyes;
  Impress on our intellects your features and voice;
  With your deathless music fill all space!

Joy of the year, friend Syāma,
Wash us and swell us with your joy;
Drive, as a current a straw,
My self before you, and open the way
Into your world of tumult and awe!
  Arouse us, great cloud,
  Impel us ahead;
  Teach us, O my bold
  Friend Syāma, the way of revolt!

The marshes sink in the glade;
The river breaks out in a glad,
Bubbling, nonsensical laughter that has made
My heart yearn only to flow with its mad
Rush round the sudden bends, under
Your grave, uncompromising thunder.
O show me that nethermost reach of the sky
Most filled with your being, most loud with your cry!

2

O uncontrollable,
As boundless and profound as the blind night!
O uncapturable,
Riding your chariot of wind to your sheer delight!
O mighty willed
Epitome of passion forever fulfilled,
     Forever unfulfilled,
What obstacle blocks the rush of your revolt,
    O warrior Syāma, high
 Priest of the summer sky?

The flood of your fury belies the boulder's powers,
Confutes the vaunted skyscraper's prowess.
You have scattered petals to the ends of the earth,
Then turned against them, crushing the soft bud's birth,
Denuding the trees of forest and grove,
And in your momentum, drove
 Pain through the shivering heart of the wild
 Bird, nested against your cold.

And yet, on the courtyards of fear you also pour
Warm rain, and courts of oppressors have heard your roar—
That urgent alarum of the spirit of revolt!

3

Now, still, dark, shapeless cloud, you solace and salve
Eyes burning and weary from too much strain
Of watching you tossing up and down on the waves
Of the tempest's swift and fickle motion—
 Now with a zeal to partake of creation,
 Now with a hot compassion for things created;
 Now crazed by the sea's immeasurable energies,
 Now playing on the soft, sane breeze.
As friend and warrior, you dazzled our eyes,
But now, childlike, you mount to the sun

Whose countless shimmering rays bow down
Before your lover's look. Effect becomes cause;
Three worlds combine in you their separate laws:
Earth, Heaven, and the Middle Space
Are one vast solace and salve to your eyes.
   Lover Syāma, the poet is bursting with new joys
At stony hardness turned tender as a flower.
   Stars by the millions praise you this hour,
               The moon, the sun, the ample skies,
               And these, our grateful and rejoicing eyes.

                                        M. HALPERN

Namvar Singh

WANDERERS

Spring. Dusk falling;
A claret mist;
Forest smells confused within the wind;
Far-off moan
Of forest stillness
Like a mute boar with a mortal wound.
Two, on foot,
Strange to each other,
Silent faces bent on the alien ground
Shadowed by Sāl trees, homelessly
Descend, descend, descend.

                                        M. HALPERN

Shamsher Bahadur Singh

DAWN

Working the daybreak,
My mind solves the night's blue-black:
  A conch shell deep in tidepool,
  Slate smeared with wet ash;
Catches now the saffron crack:
  Streak of thick, orange chalk,
  A woman's body stirring
  In a cold spring lake.
With one white stroke,
Sun rises, resolves the sky.

J. MAUCH

Naresh Kumar Mehta

TIME

Let us make this lake endure
Not by touching it
Not by sitting at its shore,
But by looking together into its mirror,
Dedicating ourselves to it,
This water,
Which is time.

J. MILES

Ramanand Doshi

EVENING

Birds returning
Through
Evening's dusk:
Birds arrayed
Aligned spread their wings
Consider tender bits of straw
Which the affectionate earth
Has placed in their nests
Consider fledglings
Whose open tiny beaks
Peer forward
Toward newest provender
Within their hearts
Thousands of unknown
Lie unexpressed.

Birds, nightborne
Express
An eagerness for home.
Nestlings await them eager eyed
. . . and memory floods through
These nestlings as through
Those in flight.
Evening is setting in.
I am alone.

What portion of the debt
My debt to mother earth

Have I left unpaid?
What, where is the balance?
I have given much. There is still much to be given.
I have taken much. There is still much to receive.
I have visited many places
But there are still many places
I must visit.

The mind is lost.
The legs are fatigued.
The path
Has been dimmed.
I have no rest, nor nestlings.
I have no companions. I am alone
The evening is setting in.

H. M. GUY

Gajanan Madhav Muktibodh

A SINGLE SHOOTING STAR

A distant star
Shoots through the blue of space.
Here, someone measures its speed,
Records the rise and set.
But nothingness of space,
Assumed to blue, must spell
An answer inaccessible
To stretching scope,
Eye muscle's strain.
Astronomers describe
Its pace and spatial shift,
Account for its time concealed

In tunnels of shade.
Yet it tracks only itself,
Oblivious to sketch
And sketcher, eye and scope.

With equal speed,
Another lone star seems
To move across the space
Of every man's heart. So,
In moving out of shades
Of evil, reining self,
Riding the void, each star
Becomes the image seeing
Its own fearless offspring—
Because of this I shall
Put faith in every man,
In every man's son.

J . M A U C H

Govinda Chandra Pande

T H E   F L O W E R S   K N O W

The flowers know their time, the sense
Of it grown in them till they bloom,
Much like our tender coming, unperceived;
They know their time and fall with it away.
Though calendars begin
Their blossoming just now,
Their warming pinks and reds,
January, one day off
From spring, has frozen in
The heart, that still alive,

[64]

Feels less for cold and less,
And then it is the cooling that it feels
        Is time, and time again
Is buried by repeated falls of snow,
And all the senses that the heart has meant
Are senseless now, but one, that knows what time
To hearken to the last, unsounded call
Of death.

L . E . N A T H A N

Makhanlal Chaturvedi

IN THE COURT OF THE GREEN GRASS

Has, in this rush of sun that's turned
The dark blue landscape green, ah has
The royal sky itself descended
To court the lowly grass?

Tall trees, their charms gaudy and shallow,
Stand unregarded, putting forth
Suppliant branches, begging a boon
From the well-favored earth.

Creepers, once radiantly strong,
Are drooping past their passing prime;
While on the grass-tips, fresh as ever,
Like pearls the dewdrops gleam.

Proud peahen, don't go trampling around
As if you owned this lowly lawn.
The gardener who sowed these pearls is envied
By even the pearl-fed swan.

Has, out of love for the humble, heaven
Exchanged its blue for green? Ah has
The royal sky itself descended
To court the lowly grass?

M . HALPERN

Ramvilas Sharma

AUTUMNAL

There, all gold spread over heaven,
The west of gold where the sun sinks,
True gold, afire by its own heat,
Millet, in sheaves, so ripe it droops.

A stick to harry in her hand,
She bends to scatter those thieving birds,
The shine on her face more gold than gold's,
Her figure laden with its own ripeness.

L . E . NATHAN

Kunwar Narayan

WINTER MORNING

Huddled in shawls of night,
Peering out timidly—light,
Just as a drowsy bird,
Stretching over its nest,
Yawned its morning song,
While further off, the squeak

Of a wheezing engine strained
To find its voice, and, coughing,
To clear, to clear, to speak
Fully out with its brazen,
Silence-needling shriek,
To make its iron version
Heard, until it, hooting,
    Hauled itself over vision.

In the mind of silence, all sound
Faded; then, silence turned,
Bored on its bed; and pulled up
Sleep to cover its head,
But doors that held in this hush
    Gave with the merest push.

High wind in the heady trees
Squandered leaves cheaply on fury,
Slapped the dew-faced blossoms,
Smarting with cold already,
While night wound away, as quick
As a spotted snake whose motion
Is the narrowest undulation
Of stealth in the thick of stalks.
The cold-blooded, shark-mouthed wind
Left in the wake of its fin
The body of the mist,
Rolling in its own shimmer,
    Slick in its bellying skin.

The rounded lull of ponds
Trembled and broke and dreams
Trembled and broke when sleep's
Blinding little lid
Lifted and lifted the dark
That preoccupied every face.

O and Neem twigs shook the air
And the air sang them till breathing
Was to drink in song so full
Body and soul were touched
    Like lovers that hear warm singing.

Cumulus, blossoming the sky,
Gathered in radiance,
Until, so heavy with colors,
The sun sank slowly on fields
Piling up delicate vapors.
Eastward where light spreads up,
Fountains lifted to rain
Warmth and sweetness, their shower
Glistening on the wet green;
The moon slipped sidelong down,
A kite, whose string snapped, falls
Into that thicket beyond.
Spinning the sky, like lambs
Winged for innocent flights,
Birds wrangled for threads of sun
    Among their high delights.

Daylight's now gold suspension
Hanging half through the dark,
And fired with sudden spite,
It stamps on the trophies raised
By defeated night, flings here,
Tosses there small pieces of dark
As one flings rags out the door
Worn out and dirtied by
    The failure who lived here before.

                    L . E . NATHAN

Nirala [Suryakant Tripathi]

STUMP

A mere stump,
All foliage gone,
Done with making.
Spring approaches and it does not quiver with anticipation.
Spring arrives and it does not bend to a bow under the
    green weight.
Nor does the love god, concealed in its branches, shoot
    from that bow
  Keen arrows carved of its pungent blossoms.
No traveller rests in its shade,
No lover weeps in the spot of shade
Cast by an old blind bird who sits there
  Dumbly recalling the music it once could make.

M. HALPERN

Ramsewak Srivastava

AROUND ME

Around the mosque
The path of night grows fragrant.
Floats on the air
The flowering queen of night.
Sounds now and then, close but invisible,
A thin, sweet voice.
Passes, morning and evening,
A lively procession of large and small squirrels.

[69]

A blue bird
  (which learned to fly
  only the other day)
Is fluttering to reach the flying kites
To touch the painted patterns
Of the clouds on sky.
It stops to hear the rising cry
Of the recitation of Krishna's dance of love,
It seeks the secret of reality.

A wild rose
Early fading
  (on every petal, the imprint
  of a finger)
Looks at morning and at evening
To every passer by, coming and going.

And I
Try to live in them,
Take failure as rehearsal,
Today as
Scenery for tomorrow.

J. MILES

Thakur Prasad Singh

FALL OF LEAVES

Leaves rain down—others will take their lost green place,
   But those who set their hearts on this spring's Sal tree
      boughs,
    What solace shall leaf their loss?
These leaves are little mouths that kiss in wind,

While human kisses have an end.
What can restore the way the young leaves were to those
   Who, after a trance of green, say "never again?"
Who shall stop the water of eyes that shone
   With pleasure, but now shine with pain?
Leaves pour down, heap on the roads their decay.

The cuckoo, now sullen, will sing a warmer day
When trails lead young feet to the shaded grass;
Fists all shall open, locked in their winter age;
Dawn shall light foreheads lifting toward a kiss.
   Heaven to make new spring, shall even sun
   On those who, numb, have lost an earlier one.

                              L. E. NATHAN

Narendra Sharma

O GREAT STAG FROM THE BAMBOO

O great stag from the bamboo,
Why have you come to amble
This city's bare avenue?

"The thicket where I thrived
Was sheltered, and tendered its green,
And I grazed on the generous grass
That was easy enough to find,

Till a young man yesterday
Strolled from here to my wood,
And though tired, his look showed a mind
Indifferent to all but his mood.

And, stalk by stalk, he hacked
My whole home down, to measure
The perfect length for one flute
And, in the waste, found his pleasure.

I've come to die for such music
Born in the ruin I knew."

O great stag from the bamboo.

L. E. NATHAN

Kedarnath Singh

SELF PORTRAIT

A line
Drawn through this globe
And all its latitudes
Loses itself
Near orbit of the sun—
At that point, there am I.

A fisherman's net
Drawn from a river
And draped on my brute shoulders—
This is my town.

Smiles
Suspended from an arch on strings
Sway towards my home.
When stirred by wind.

My house is small.
Within that house
Are countless speeding lines
And each line touches others quickly.
There, where they meet,
There I am.

W . M . M U R R A Y

Paramanand Srivastava

SEASIDE INN, EVENING

At this sallow inn,
    hard by the beach,
        night slyly
    has secreted me . . .

In a corner,
        dark or maybe half
That dark,
And somewhat
Served by
Wisps of savor,
Served by
Unrequested music
Ordering the air,
Served by
Stillness, drawn through
Fog to miles of thinness . . .
From here the city blinks
    like a nervous star.

L . E . N A T H A N

[73]

Ajit Kumar

. . . But the accursed twilight came,
Brought with it the bad spirits of past memories
And a shabby dusk.

All of a sudden, as if wet fuel started smoking,
As if that sort of smoke rose up from the houses
In a spiral, with a dark hazy line behind it,
Mind and eyes burned with bitter tears.

This twilight, with somewhere a patch of light
But mostly darkness prevailing,
Increases, as if building a fence of giant size
For a giant with no heart.
I feel that my life is in a cage,
And outside, tigers, bears, wild dogs—
Memories, hurts, fears—
Surround me,
My life inextricably set
In the accursed twilight.

J . M I L E S

Kesari Kumar

EVENING

Evening
Is, well,
The yawn of a rude guest
Who, in company,
Slams his eyes shut,
Raises his hairy arms
As one would raise the shaggy boughs of a tree
And snap his fingers—
Ho-hum——
Snaps his fingers like, well, like winding necks
Of famished baby birds tangled
Above their nest.

Or else
A high-strung girl
Who sails pages of books, torn out and folded,
As one would set loose
Butterflies,
Or who digs at a heavenly print with the wrong end
Of a pen; punching through a cloud mass
To meet red eyes staring her down
Till she hides her face in her dusty skirt
And sobs.

Or else
Is a sopping
Blotter that returns for new black an old red,
Old red for new black in inky mingling of both,

And reverses the signatures it presses
In this useless bringing together
And muddled oneness.
No, I'm not in the mood yet
To give up.

Light will loaf against the horizon,
And on the dizzy peaks,
The Kanchanjangha,
Around the unseen back slope
Of Ramgiri, the home
Of Kalidasa's alienated love,
The cloud will be clowning like a lecherous elephant.

No, I'm in no mood to end.
Now
Great dancer,
Shiva
Dance,
Dance on the corpse.

L . E . N A T H A N

Vishwanath

THE FAMILY

My father,
   a conquered Everest,
My mother,
   an ocean of milk poisoned by poverty.
My brother,
   a lion cub cinched up as a pack animal,
My sister,

a doll made out of soiled clothes,
And I,
   a kettle of water
   steaming away to vapor,
   water consumed into vapor.

J . MILES

Shri Kant Varma

TRACT AGAINST TRACT HOUSES

House against house for miles of repetition;
In each, a stranger faces walls so dense
That all doors open on someone's isolation,
Shadow darkening shadow closing down,
Till only the sky windows a failing light;
These lower windows shutter all want in—
No open hand, no fist, no love, no hate.
The heron cries for those who can't reveal
How meaningless is all unmated hurt.

House against house: how can the tenants feel
Their way through crowds that cannot live apart?
Morning yawns the door of every cave;
Evening crumbles into black; but noon
Is numb, a vast and slowly sinking wave
Of heat over the huddle of the town
That in its daze is helpless: unnerved hand,
Powerless to flex, to lift, to touch,
To proffer, or to hold. Dead on the land
It sprawls.
         Struggling up, a raw new hutch
Leans on an old one as towns multiply,

But is this birth? I've heard no claiming wail
Of new-come rage or pain or joy—no cry
That calls for blessing on this sweating soil.

L. E. NATHAN

Agyeya [Sachchidananda Vatsyayan]

JET FLIGHT

Not through heaven but unformed light.
Wing-balanced and cut loose
From gravity,
We glide.
New-combed cloud fleece
Is spread below us, dream of white
And impossibly delicate cloth.
Here I think I dream my own solidity.

And there
Through the torn floor of cumulus,
Is it earth I really see—
Those lines, trailing through green or shade or light,
Or angling, crossing, curving, driving straight?
Then, like a jewel, cresting man's own crown,
The city shapes, and laboring spires,
Memorialize this creature who creates.

Losing pure altitude,
We burrow under smog,
That drab and dirty tissue in which works
A suffocating womb of mobbed plenitude.
At bottom,
Now, we touch

The hard earth
Where blood grows weighty
In the veins and this most urgent ring,
Just behind the ear drums, sings
The desolate dumbness of our being.

Descend a further step,
Breathe deep;
Close up the silver dream,
Our casket-chariot behind;
Step down, then stroll,
And there before you stands,
Unpredictable, your image:
Man, from whose eyes, his own Unbounded Self's
            Unblinking grief stares out.

                    L . E . N A T H A N

Govinda Chandra Pande

P R E   L U N I C A

On a path to the moon,
Unwearied, alone,

            A moon-mad hound
            Lifts a long moan
            From the desolate ground
                    Up to the moon.

The still ground stretches
Away to where
The still sky reaches
            Up to the moon.

[79]

Now silent, the hound
Stretches to hear
What answering sound
May reach his ear
     From the silent moon.

M. HALPERN

Kedar Nath Agrawal

AGAINST FLUTE PLAYING

Boatman, your flute song hurts! My heart is beaten,   1.1.1
Beaten up as waters are stirred, is beaten
As waters beaten up by ships that cleave them.

Boatman, your flute song pierces! My promise is broken,
Is snapped as dry grass, trampled on, is broken,
When woods in dry savannahs seem forsaken.

Boatman, enough, enough! Song sways my being,
Sways as you sway, until my whole swayed being
Becomes the boatman, drifting, fluting, shaken.

L. E. NATHAN

Bachchan [Harivansh Rai]

MY GARDEN PLANT

My garden plant, my friend, my likeness,
Plant of my garden,
You bear within you the plant of my being,
Friend of my being.

My being's beloved sowed you,
My garden thrived on the wealth of your being,
My garden plant, my friend, my likeness,
Friend of my being,
Emblem of him I have loved.
Ah how shall I water you now?
My pitcher of love is empty,
My likeness, my friend,
My garden plant, my friend, my likeness,
Plant of my being,
Plant of my love, my likeness, my being,
My garden friend.

Now is the month of the great monsoon,
But he I have loved is away, is away,
All I have been is passing away,
My garden plant, my friend, my likeness,
Plant of my garden.
How dry your leaves now, your stalk
How dry, how hardened;
The song in my throat now hurts, being hardened and dry,
My garden plant, my likeness, my friend.

[81]

May the last of my being be laid
In the shade of your being,
May God endow me with power to endure past love,
    My garden plant, my friend, my likeness,
    Plant of my garden,
    Who bear within you the plant of my being,
    Friend of my being.

M . HALPERN

Bhagwan Prasao Singh

YOUR GLANCE

Your glance
Touched mine and drooped
As rose petals
Heavy in full bloom
Hang without breaking

Whiffed through my mind
As rose fragrance
Heavy in the air
Scents without spreading

Filled in my heart
As bunched roses
Heavy in a bowl
Swell without crowding.

J . MAUCH

Malati Parulkar

The path,
Now libertine, now holding the straight and narrow,
Now drowsing in the hills' protective shade,
Follows the ways of its whims,
Fondling tree trunks,
Stretching and yawning on plains,
Strolling demurely through meadows.
It thrills to the tickle of spray from the spouting falls
And to the closing eyes of the wild flowers
That sway seductively on the heights above;
But when it comes to the real thing, it is shy
As the mouth of the virgin bride.
Who knows what sound of what song can rouse it to
    passion?

Collector of fragrances, musics, and sorrows
From leaf and flower,
From river banks,
From dew-bright soil,
From heaped up pebbles that give off
Odor for none but itself,
From rain-water flooding the grassy slopes
Or dripping down from the eaves;
From wheatfield, maizefield, rice-paddy spread to the sky;
In the morning it powders its face with motes of sunlight,
And, peeping whenever it can in some lucid pond,
Admires its varied reflections.

Once in a while, at the dark of the moon,
Or when the full moon shines like day on the dew of the
    fields,
It will leap the horizon to pilfer a kiss from the moon;
Or sometimes, without rhyme or reason,
Will set itself at the head of a wind on the distant sky.
It has a way of seducing the traveller
Into such a strange sweet longing,
That whether it be day or night
No longer concerns him;
And on and on he journeys,
Rapt in that dream which drove him out on the path,
Unable to barter his aspirations at any price,
Unbroken even by gallows,
Unstopping even when his destination is reached,
Possessed by some terrible truth
Of which he can never be deprived.

M. HALPERN

Bhavaniprasad Misra

BALLAD OF DESOLATION

First you must hear my name,
Then this address that I whisper,
And don't be shocked, by the by,
If I ask you a little favor.

Deluded ones call me Quiet;
Others Dumbness; some Keep Still;
I am none of these, for I have
Voices enough at my will.

Something stirs in me often,
Or a glow when I am alight;
A frog might have budged or a glow-worm
Deceived you with its flight.

Though desolate, I speak;
Though immobile, I can move too;
This murmur is mine, and this flutter,
Secrets I commit to you.

I live alone, so alone
That only long grasses endure,
Tamarind and Pepal trees
Double the darkness here.

You find me here where I stand
Or, lying, take my ease;
I have chosen ruin, for I
Was nurtured in places like these.

And on this castle wall
And courtyard there is a watch,
The outposts of superstition
Worsening with their touch.

Although no place lacks some terror,
I swear there is little to fear,
Only a minor thing maybe . . .
The people who used to be here.

Once in this place lived a queen;
The records have skipped her story:
She was mad for a breakneck lover;
That was her single folly.

[85]

This ramshackle landing at the river,
This poor heap of rotten planks,
Was where the madcap sang;
It's ages since he sat on these banks.

Evenings, at her window,
The queen repeated his notes;
Then he'd come play to her only,
And, hiding, she'd sing with his flute.

The king at last saw it all,
And his heart contracted with pain;
Ablaze with fury, he asked
What those evenings had meant to the queen.

And the queen cried, "Call him here;
I'm mad! Forget me! I long,
Awakened all day, my lord,
To be put to sleep by his song."

He was a king and could not
Suffer so rash a reply;
The queen had answered as though
There was no prison nearby.

Where you stand, a gibbet was raised
And the delicate queen hanged there,
And there, of course, her madcap;
The king laughed, "It was her error."

But after, he did not laugh,
For the lover's song was still heard
And at times, "My lord, *your* error,"
Were the dead queen's taunting words.

Years passed and palace halls,
Emptied by ruin, grew still,
And then I came with my friends
And we do just as we will.

But suddenly the madcap and queen
Return, and their singing makes
The air sweat strange terror for
My lizards, my owls, and my snakes.

L. E. NATHAN

Paramanand Srivastava

I CALL TO MIND TODAY

I call to mind today
Many views
And objects
Each unrelated to the other
And self-ignoring.

A flowing river
And a swimming sky
An opening window
And a low-toned tune.

The river is not the one
To be seen from your roof,
The sky is not the one ever floating
At the rim of your courtyard,
The window is not the one
Which opens in your room,

And the tune not the one
Played by your fingers.

I do not know why I am so eager
To relate these views and objects to your name,
Views and objects unrelated
And self-ignoring.

J. MILES

Nirala [Suryakant Tripathi]

THE STREAM OF LOVE

The stream of love has veered away,
Leaving the self a sand-bed, dry
As twigs of a dead Mango tree which complains:
"No cuckoo or peacock will come again.
For gone are my flowers and fruits: my fresh
Spring radiance has withered to ash
Which the wind scatters."
                    I am a line of a song
Gone stale but still insistent. No longer
Do single moments glow with a glow of forever,
Like those when I and my loved one sat together
On the green, moonlit bank of that full
Stream that has changed its course. Now all
Is moonless night, I am lost and alone.
So said the poet,
              and having said, is gone.

M. HALPERN

Kedar Nath Agrawal

THE RIVER

The river is a girl of pleasure
Down from the hills to show her treasure:
Thighs that she turns out at her leisure
And swans that tread them to love's measure;
The Devil made her such a teaser.
Trees, like crazy boys, whole days here,
Hang around and dance to please her,
Bend for kisses to her pleasure.

The river is an unsheathed blade,
Flashing in the wide green glade,
Edge the keenest ever made,
Tempered with the lightning's aid,
Quick as devils to evade;
While banks, its bearers, unafraid,
Deftly grasp what they wouldn't trade
For life itself without this blade.

L. E. NATHAN

Dharmavir Bharati

EVENING CLOUDS

Caravels on the unmapped river
Hoist their sails,
Sleeves of magi,
As they glide over,
Slowly.

Keels of emerald,
Decks awash

[89]

With marigolds—
Without a helmsman,
Unrigged they run,
With cargos of coral and vermillion.

From far and near
They listing come
With rare lumber,
Sandalwood,
Blocks of camphor,
Casks of orange ochre,
Silk in bales,
Or a dream of nets
In tangled piles.

L. E. NATHAN

Namvar Singh

EVENING LOOMS

Evening looms
On the hills ahead;
A voice calls from the waterfall behind.
There, under the arc
Of the myriad spray,
Something I've left sends after me the sound
Of a child's cry.
Two minds, both drowning
In the same stream, collided, each one blind
To the other. Do
You recall how I watched
Those eyes afloat on a face a half-moon round?
Like a broken bangle, that face clasps on my mind.

M. HALPERN

Kedarnath Singh

FOG

Two paths now flow through shade: below, earth's trail,
And over it, the white way of the mist;
Now, birds who drank the wind for song are shaken,
Their long melodic line fearfully broken;
I, with that breaking line of geese, now sail
Into my final moment, fully blessed,
While trees, wells, houses, doors sink in a pale
    And soft gray ocean,
Swirling backward like my hopeless past—
    A formless motion.

Torn on the branches, rags and wisps of sun
Weakly flutter as the leaves spin down,
Till very emptiness calls out to me,
Although ahead the paths have lost their way,
And breathing sodden air too deeply aches,
And the heart, naked in the twilight, shivers;
But, fresh from autumnal ripening, earth first takes
    The winter's sudden shock
As haze smothers the shy gloom of the lakes
    And night blots rivers.

Their thin hands so untimely frozen, clocks
Now nurse no more the minutes, hours, quarters.

L. E. NATHAN

Agyeya [Sachchidananda Vatsyayan]

A MOMENT ON GREEN GRASS

Let us sit on the green grass
Here on this slope.
There won't be any gardeners or watchmen around now.
And the grass is ever spread out green,
Ever inviting itself to be trampled by anyone—
So like the open feelings of our generation.

Come sit here, a little closer;
Leave room only for love:
Puff away the air of modern propriety.

Speak aloud
Or in a whisper
Or speak within yourself
Or keep silent,
But be only you:
Not stiff and strained like that picket fence.
Bend, reach with a natural grace,
Bloom in a smile that stems
From the roots of restraint,
From within, like the grass.
We may for a moment
Forget the ceaseless babble of the town
And not think being here an escape;
We may for a moment
Look upon the sky, the earth, the clouds,
Green grass,
Plants, the dangling vines,

[92]

Flowers,
Leaves falling,
Butterflies and gnats,
The vain small bird, on a twig, raising its tail.
And guilt will not snap at us,
"Folly, Love of nature is folly:
This is the age of the People."

We may for a moment
Not exist,
Or, even if we exist,
We may for a moment
Be absorbed into the echo of a quick wave
Flattening on the shore of a distant sea
In our heart's solitude,
A sea in which we are miniscule,
Like a pair of oysters.
Allow for a moment
Neither you nor I
Nor doubt of something greater.

We may for a moment
Recall automatically
A boat plying on the river,
The first showers of July
Spattering on a dusty path,
Swimming together in the lake,
Unprovoked laughter beneath the banyan tree,
Your sunburned face, lines of your hair
Fixed on the face by beads of sweat,
Pine forest, two horses running together,
The wind soaked with the river,
Gasping for breath,
The steamer's sad whistle,
Temple ruins,
Fingers interwoven,
Honey right from the comb,

[93]

The approaching pat of the postman's feet,
The dusty smell of the half-known acacia tree,
Silken tassels of the Shirisha tree lying in the dust,
Lines of the poem,
The sun dropping behind the dome of the mosque,
Glossy rocks by the spring,
Peacock with its mate,
Anklets,
The pain-tense, slow-opening measure of the Santhali Song,
The train coasting with a sigh,
Waves,
Rainstorm,
A hand's width of shade on the sand beneath the shrub,
A tiny rick of strawpieces, each cut to a finger's length.
Hot wind.
Silence.

We recall without effort.
We do not think.
We are running for the shelter of the past.
But let us not retrogress;
Let us not huddle in the corner of the past.

Come, sit
For a moment,
A moment not donated through the generosity of the town
    merchants,
Reckon this moment as interest on our own capital of
                                        life.

Come, sit,
So I may for a moment
Look upon your face,
Revert to each lineament
Of the face, of the eyes—
Of the mind,
Of the thousand memories we share.

I see all in fine lineation,
In such a way that no guilt yaps at my heels.

Slowly, slowly,
Those lines will fade into the solvent darkness;
Only your eyes will shine out.
Slowly, slowly,
Each leaf of the green grass will flicker out at the
                              hedges' feet,
And the hedges themselves fade into the looming
                         darkness of the horizon.
Let there remain only undefined expansion,
Freedom realized: all openness.

Let's get up and move.
Till now we were friends.
Come for a walk.
(Did you see the Satbhaiya birds playing on the grass?).
If we stay longer, Someone might say,
"Look at the lovers huddling in the dark."
Even if we are,
Let only the green grass know it
(The acquiescent grass that has been trampled by everyone
Because it invites everyone).

Let's not hear talk about lovers
From the people of the town,
Whose words are like gluey soap,
Sterile of compassion.

Let's get up and move.

J. MAUCH

Navin [*Balakrishna Sharma*]

A drop drew out of the ocean, toward the moon's height,
Began pulling between small finite, great infinite.

Forsook its vast source, then became
Minuscule, infinitesimal particle.
Immovable, succumbed to laws of motion,
Colored and cast by wind in shape and form,
                    Left the ocean.

Rode a thundering and roaring force
Across the sky, cherished the notion
To measure space and time; this silly one
Drew away from its own immeasurable home;
                    Left the ocean.

Turned vapor and globe of dew,
Sharp frost, soft rain, iota of contentment
Moment of Catak's fulfillment. But where its depth?
It felt the press of living outside itself
                    When it left the ocean.

Wandered the sky, entered the center of earth,
Watered roots of trees, nectared flowers,
Counted out endless time, up and down,
But could not for a moment forget its home.
                    After it left the ocean.

O deep ocean of affection, O distant moon
Of fulfillment, the vain drop now
Shatters. Existence outside self is untenable.
Come storming around me now; ages have gone
                Since I left the ocean.

J . MILES

Nirala [Suryakant Tripathi]

AT THE LANDING

Not here, friend! Moor us anywhere, but not
Here! The whole town would stare, seeing this boat
Made fast to the ferry landing near the spot
Where *she* was wont to bathe. Here have I seen,
Eyes fastened and legs trembling, those limbs that shone
Rising out of the wavelets, those eyes ashine
Over a smile which said so much, yet all
And always to itself—that listening smile,
Amused, indulgent toward whatever it heard,
While to a secret inner landing tightly moored.

M . HALPERN

Trilochan Shastri

Estimable anguish
Kept its dominion over me.

The ocean floor
Is not regular,
Far and deep in some places, and in some
Shallow and near.

But sands exposed and bare,
Spread by ocean tides,
Lie wide and desolate
Beyond estimate.

J . MILES

Prabhakar Machwe

A SHORT TREATISE ON LOVE

Is love a beggar whose touch is tepid?
       Love is a cascading,
       Restlessly singing,
       Day and night ringing.
Love is an archer, lost to himself, missing his target.
       Love is delighted
       Though fields are blighted
       And famine foresighted.
Creating tiller, helpless in grain where he lords it.

L . E . NATHAN

Kunwar Narayan

INTERROGATION

Impertinent laughter echoes
through the blind alleys of the stars:
This is my question . . .
Among such immense paraphernalia
a big snowman is melting
at the redhot point of the needle
of my piercing inquiry . . .
Was this your answer?

H. M. GUY

Shamsher Bahadur Singh

MORNING

The rock
That was crouched
On a shelf
Awoke
And automatically
Stretched
Itself.

J. MAUCH

Dushyanta Kumar

THE CONTINUAL BURNING

The red, the hot incendiary
Touched me off on fire, O, everywhere—
Sent up tomorrow like a flare,
Smoldered in yesterday's dark air,
Withered seed, sprout, bush, whole tree,
Blossom, leaf, and fruit in its glare;
The wind that had come to cool
Crackled hotly through my hair.

Not one instant untouched
By this fire's sweeping brand;
Like impotent water I boiled
In time's old kettle
That bubbles to no end.

A quarter of my life
Boiled off continuously like this,
Squandered in vapor, fading,
Wandering lost
In space that voided me into its nothingness.

What pleasure is this continual boiling over
In which thought cannot rise, lidded by torpor?
 O let some sensible shape take place in heat.
If fire must be, let it consume complete,
So the tempestuous boil will vaporize
And I, martyr of new meaning, rise,
The heavy lid suddenly flung off,
And, motion's spirit, I find my perfect size.
Now, let the fire continue burning
And let the water of this life keep turning.

L. E. NATHAN

[100]

Shambhunath Singh

SEARCH FOR DIRECTIONS

Those directions may be mine
Where I've not gone,
Where I've not strung my crown
With every fragrant bead
Of dew, petal, and bud.
Those places may be mine,
Mine alone.

Those directions may be mine
Where unheard sound
Leaves traces on the wind,
Where reveries
Sparkle with truth;
Each solitary lane,
Each unsniffed breeze,
Each empty path—
Those directions may be mine,
Mine alone.

Those directions may be mine
Where the blind stallion Time
Is tied to the stem
Of the Pepal tree of heaven;
Where earth is ripped by his hooves,
Whose day and night,
Hours, minutes, seconds pulsate
Away like waves;
Where sun and moon
Neither rise nor set

But shine with a black light
And bright shadow on the stone,
That which may be all mine,
Mine alone.

Such directions may be mine.

J. MAUCH

Prabhakar Machwe

FRAGMENTS OF DOUBT

The solitude questions the waterfall's continual babbling;
The asking of trees is put by the birds' wild mocking;
Hint of more asking is in the rainbow's arching;
I've brought two fragments of doubt in the bag of my
knowing.

L. E. NATHAN

Navin [Balakrishna Sharma]

MY HOUSE IS AFIRE

My God, my house is afire, it is ablaze.
Someone breathes in my ear, O senseless, awake, awake.
I am indolently lying down, stretching my legs.
Shutting my eyes to the huge loss I will take.
All that is mine being consumed while I wait for aid.
Even now this my mind will not shake
Off. Someone breathes in my ear, Awake, awake.

[102]

The fire of desire, the fire of wrath is ablaze
Here the fire of rancor, there of hate,
The volcano is smoking, the ground has been shaken away,
My foes throw colors of flame from the bonfires they make
In my house. My house is afire, ablaze.

Should I say that these fire-makers are foes or friends?
Without their presence, human meaning ends.
They make me shudder in their fiery ways.
My white swan's mind blackens, chars to a crow's.
O my house is afire, it is ablaze, ablaze.

J . MILES

Sumitra Nandan Pant

MIND BURNS

How the mind burns!
All night, moments igniting moments show
How the mind burns,

How body and mind become one,
How thought when it burns composes to body,
How, atom
By rising atom,
The body and mind become one.

This body-mind is what sees and hears;
In public and private, gives and takes.
The pain and pleasure bound up in being.
But when it flies to the bounds of Being
And, all besmirched with desire, returns
To hover as blithe as a rainbowed cloud
In the sky of my particular being,
Who is to say how this happens, or how

That cloud, bursting, can shower rays of light?
In, out, up, down, coming and going,
The play of its shadows composes and decomposes
Into the shadowless One. But how?
Is it that, buried in this body-mind,
Endures, forever burning, the flame of soul
Whose light is the life of those shadow-plays?

Who is to say? Only the give and take
Answers my hows and whats and what nots.
For what is knowing? Who is the knower who knows?
In-out, out-in, the mind still moves.

How the mind burns!
How, in the raging flux of the body-mind,
The Conscious and Unconscious form, re-form,
Re-form, form. Forming and re-forming,
How the mind burns!

M . H A L P E R N

Raghuvir Sahae

IMPRESSIONS OF WATER

Lightning flash.
Rains pour down in a dense forest far off.
Noon: dark lake: a branch of mango drooping over it.
Breeze: I stand by the window . . . and the spray
Of the breeze has touched me.
Suddenly night: sand suddenly upon the other side,
Suddenly a calm, deep river
Comes into sight.
. . . So water leaves its many marks
Upon the mind.

H . M . G U Y

Nirala [Suryakant Tripathi]

EXILE

Alone let me walk this path of exile, alone.
My own fruits let me harvest, on my own.
       Weathers within have flung me down—
       Tempest of blood, earthquake of bone;
       And now the fever I caught from my own
       Iniquities, I would cure, but alone.
Where else but down this straight path can I find
That moment emptied of doubt, that place where the mind
Has unsuffered its past? I would put the past behind
By bearing present pain and joy, but alone.

M. HALPERN

Maithili Sharan Gupta

NOW, THOSE DAYS ARE GONE FOR GOOD

Now, those days are gone for good.
      Though heart's sap swells in us still,
It is body's once stout trunk
      that, drained so, lacks will.

Rains rode by and left their stamp of lightning;
      winter withdrew and left us with its chill;
Leaving behind their sulky heats for remembrance,
      how many springs have crossed the barren hill?

Only God knows whether
       the gaming meant gain or loss for our skill,
but who can gainsay one win?
       Songs gone for good, their echoes lift us still.

L. E. NATHAN

Kedarnath Singh

NEW DAY AT MY DOOR

Someone
Has laid this new day at my door
Like a letter bearing a strange and distant postmark,
Its virginal envelope sealed
With a sign of auspicious turmeric.
Come, let me break the seal.

Come, do not hesitate; open and read.
This errant message must not go,
Like so many others before it, unheeded.
Here, in this tremulous morning light,
It waits on your doorstep, calm and quiet,
Inviting, asking you to know
Its secret—golden secret of a blossoming day.
O do not delay!

But a small question like a nagging child
Comes prattling along the street and grasps my hand.
Who knows
What language waits within?
Who knows for certain whose
Message was laid in the ghostly hours before dawn
At the wrong door? I do not find

[106]

My own address.
No, nor my name. Alas,
How dare I break the seal?

This hand
Which opened the door, opened horizons in all directions.
Why does it hesitate now on the verge of revelation?
Why
Not break this auspicious seal of a new sun's rays?
God only can say.

M . HALPERN

Shamsher Bahadur Singh

SENILE LIGHT

The body of evening
    as if poised in breathless meditation . . .
The heart
    coming to the conclusion of its motion . . .
The senile light
    now in the calm of its humiliation.

L . E . NATHAN

Kedar Nath Agrawal

STORM

Like a stallion
I raced cantering over the heads of the forest.
Like a young bird
The biggest tree was startled and shrieked aloud.
Violently trembling, the feathery leaves were ripped off.
Broken, as if the wild bulls of the plateau
Had been set out to feed upon the dark green twigs
Of the silent night.

H. M. GUY

Sarveshwar Dayal Saksena

YOU HAVE LOST YOUR WAY

When I went barefoot people loved me.
As long as my dwellings were banks and fields,
Human affection clung to me
As moist sod clung to my toes and heels.

But then, when I got me some socks and shoes,
And watched and worried my pocketbook,
The near and dear who had wandered with me
Picked up and left, with averted looks.

[108]

From breezy slopes to the warehouse's stench
I traced the narrowing path of my loss,
Watching the dews on the violet
Evaporate in the fire of remorse.

I turned to a haunter of darkest alleys,
Seeking some clue to your new address,
A watcher of lights in the city night
At every window of every house.

I took to reading nameplates by matchlight,
Rubbing each dusty letter clear;
I took to opening gates in the fences
Of fenced-off dwellings, till the door

Would open, and someone's scathing voice
Cry, "No one you want is here, go away!"
Each slamming door, each light turned out
Cried, "They are gone, you have lost your way."

M. HALPERN

Navin [*Balakrishna Sharma*]

FEVER IS LOOKING THROUGH MY EYES

Friend, fever is looking through my eyes.
Mind is restless, body burns and sighs.
Sinews of cerebral nerves split at the ends
As if wild beasts had pulled them apart. Friends
Could counsel me with "Life will make amends,"
But I am without counsel, without human ties.
Friend, fever is looking through my eyes.

Lying beneath this bitter Neem tree,
I am glad that the fever troubles only me.
And glad at least that through inflamed eyes
Tears flow, flow unceasingly.

Friend, fever is looking through my eyes.
My eyes are swollen and red from looking out
For you everywhere, and when they see you are not
Here, they brim with tears. When will it come about
That you feast them, dilate them with your sweet
Presence? Fever is looking through my eyes.

Ears hear without meaning, breath is in chaos,
Every nerve is dumb, a yearning cries
And body shivers like a willow. Who lays
Cool hands on this heated head, whose cool palm tries
To soothe it?
　　　　Friend, fever is looking through my eyes.

J . MILES

Ramdhari Singh Dinkar

THE MIRROR

You're going to the temple?
Do me a favor then:
Please take this mirror
And put it in your flower-basket.

First please your Lord, and do
As he'd want it—
With incense, fruit, and flowers—

But when he asks of the earth,
Set the mirror in front of him,

Because that glass reflects
The dreadful whirl-pool
In man's primordial mind,
The ancient dance of earth and sky.

So too will it show him
An edgeless shadow: earth's
Desire, her restless fever,
The agony of shuddering skies.

Yes, the mirror will show
The images of towers
And walls collapsing,
Of lacy melodies
Swept off forever by the wind.

Even more, it will reflect
The spectre of false Orpheus,
who clutches dying song—
No, the lyre's very corpse—
And who lies curled
Asleep in the shade of ignorance.

Your Lord will have to see
The lamb-like puffs of wind
Panicked by a storm's
Rotting skies,
And driven to bits in the onslaught.

It will force him to stare
Into the guts of the earth,
Into the flickering ash

Of dying nations,
Into the frozen knots
Of self-consumptive thought,
Dying in a waste of learning.

But stay a minute longer;
There's more for him to see:
A quick glance at the edge
Reveals a narrow light,
Now thread-like, a beginning,
A distant shining rope of gold.

Now the old bark drops off;
Green shoots sprout forth;
Torn curtains are pulled back;
A new heaven prepares to come.

J . MAUCH

Malayaj [Bharat Varma]

STATEMENT OF SOLITUDE

I am a meagre moment in the flow
Of the flooding river of your orphaned moments,
An algebraic symbol robbed of significance
In the calculus of your lingering frustration.

I am the interval
Between sting and pain,
Or a rejected particle of the future
In which you are killer and I the killed.

I am the seeping poison of the blister
Which you call art,
In the infected flush of sentimentality.

It is unbearable,
This mud bespattered rebellious sky—
Why not choke me off?

J . MILES

Agyeya [*Sachchidananda Vatsyayan*]

ISLANDS IN THE RIVER

Call us islands in the River,
Mother of turn, cape, and contour;
Her hands so shape and hold us forever—
Because the River is, we are.

We are islands and not of the current:
Our place is permanent. The instant
We flow, we are sand; we are non-existent.
But the stream is ever insistent,
And should we lose ourselves in the torrent,
Grain by grain, in unwilling decrement,
We would turn the water muddy,
Turbid and bitter, because we are present.

Call us islands, you do not curse us;
This is fate for everyone of us.
In her lap our Mother holds us,
As she is held by the Land, our Father.
She is the link between us.

Flow, then, River, enrich us
With the takings from the Land;
With our heritage, Mother, touch us.

If by your own bounty or in torment
Of constriction, you rise up
And overflow with a violent
Sweep that destroys the shape of our past—
With even that we could contend.
Wherever we are sent
We would start again as sediment,
Rise once more as impertinent bars;
And to those, Mother, you form the final
                            increment.

                            J. MAUCH

Govinda Chandra Pande

EVENING, SMALL HOUSES,
PLANTAIN TREES

Evening spreading like so much smoke,
The day sealing this hour
                    on the lake's deep.
The silvered taste pencils a picture,
                    a peeking moon.
Houses of cards build around, umbrellas of palms,
                    long, broad oyster leaves open,
Arms thicken and droop.

                            L. E. NATHAN

Kedarnath Singh

YOU ARE UTTERLY CLEAR

You are utterly clear to my seeing through
to the utmost edge of seeing:
A little squirrel's
fountaining tail,
a clutch of color adrift in the air,
a trail stabbing like a whistle's note
piercing its path through everything,
beyond everything—
so much I can see:
bridges,
fairs,
towns on the way,
and edgewise kites, cutting the sky,
yet beyond even that—
the same untiring footpath slenderly
trotting ahead, turning at turns,
striding up, striding down,
and then, live as the wiry light of lightning,
suddenly ahead, ahead, and ahead!

L. E. NATHAN

Agyeya [Sachchidananda Vatsyayan]

BORROW IN THE MORNING, LEND AT NIGHT

When I woke to morning, I saw a wealth of sun,
As a bird-song faded, its singing just done.

Sunlight I asked: Can you spare a spark of your heat?
Bird I asked: Can you lend a sweet note of your song?
Grass I inquired of: Can I beg a blade of new green?
Conch-weed I conjured: Can I share one beam of your
    opening brightness?
Wind I pleaded with: Can I take from your flowing a
    shadow of breath?
Wave I questioned: Can I have a hair's-width of your heady
    leap?
Sky I asked: Can I borrow your boundlessness for the space
    of one wink?

All, I asked for a share and all gave,
And I live, for living, in fact, adds only to these:
Warm sweetness, fragrant green opening brightness, heady,
    resilient flowing

In boundless being, aware
Of all such borrowed goods.

Dark in the desolate night, I woke from a dream
Of an Unseen Shapeless who had questioned me closely:
Your life, he said, is a heap of happenings,
Such a wide wealth,

Can't you lend me, therefore, a little of love which I swear
I'll have back with a hundredfold interest,
A hundred times that, whenever I return?

I replied: Love? Division?
My tone was tangled, for the deal
Figured far ahead of my having lived it.

That Unseen Shapeless cried: Yes,
For truly these things together form love:
This being alone, this anguish, this wanting,
This labyrinth, this lack of having been through,
This hunting, this doubleness, this helpless hurt of divorce,
This rising in dark to recognize finally
Whatever you own is owned at once by another.
It is yours, all yours,
So lend me a little
Who desire it so direly.

But in that midnight pitch of the dark, I was dumb,
Leery of lending
This Unseen Shapeless anything.
Who can tell
What this beggar may be?

L. E. NATHAN

⋖§ABOUT THE AUTHORS§⋗

As it is customary in Hindi to refer to writers by their given names rather than their surnames, this list has been put in alphabetical order according to the first name. In the case of writers who use the pen-name exclusively (it is sometimes used along with the name), the list has followed the the practice of giving the full name in brackets after the pen-name.

AGYEYA [SACHCHIDANANDA HIRANANDA VATSYA-YAN], b. 1911. Has published six volumes of verse, three novels, and several volumes of short stories and of essays. Has edited two major anthologies of modern Hindi poetry as well as several volumes of new writing by younger writers. Spent several years in prison and detention during the Indian Independence movement. During the second World War served on the Burma front. Has worked with All India Radio as lexicographer and language adviser. Was Visiting Professor, University of California, Berkeley. Now resides in New Delhi.

AJIT KUMAR, b. 1933. Has published a volume of poems and one of poems and essays. Was for some time in the Hindi Section in the Ministry of External Affairs, Government of India. Is now teaching Hindi literature in a Delhi college.

BACHCHAN [HARIVANSH RAI], b. 1907. Has published over a dozen volumes of verse. Educated at Allahabad and Banaras, "Bachchan" taught English literature at Allahabad University for some years before taking his Ph.D. from Cambridge (on a study of William Butler Yeats). Is currently Officer on Special Duty, Hindi Section, Ministry of External Affairs, Government of India, New Delhi.

[119]

BHAGWAN PRASAO SINGH, b. 1932. Has published poems and short stories in various literary journals. Teaches Hindi at Delhi.

BHAVANIPRASAD MISRA, b. 1913. Has published two volumes of verse. Spent three years in prison during the Independence movement. Besides teaching Hindi, has written songs and dialogues for films and has been a producer for All India Radio. Is now an editor of the definitive edition of Gandhi's writings being published by the Publications Division, Government of India.

DHARMAVIR BHARATI, b. 1926. Has written fiction as well as verse. Published three volumes of poems, two verse plays, two novels, and two volumes of essays. Took his Ph.D. in Hindi literature from Allahabad, where he also lectured for a few years. Is now Editor of the *Weekly Dharmayug*, Bombay.

DUSHYANTA KUMAR, b. 1933. Has published a volume of poems and contributed to several literary journals. Was for some time with All India Radio as an Assistant Producer. Is now Assistant Director, Language Department, Madhya Pradesh, Bhopal.

GAJANAN MADHAV MUKTIBODH (1917–1964). Besides contributing to literary journals, has published two volumes of poems and a book of critical essays. Was teaching Hindi literature at the Digvijay College in Rajnandgaon (Madhya Pradesh). Died after a prolonged illness in Delhi.

GOVINDA CHANDRA PANDE, b. 1923. Professor of Ancient Indian History and Culture at Gorakhpur University and now at the University of Jaipur. Has published *Studies in the Origins of Buddhism*. Poems have appeared in various literary journals.

KEDAR NATH AGRAWAL, b. 1911. Has published three volumes of verse and contributed to literary journals. Been prominently associated with the "progressive" school in Hindi poetry. Practices law in Banda, Uttar Pradesh.

KEDARNATH SINGH, b. 1932. Has published a volume of poems and a critical study of the symbolist movement in modern Hindi poetry. Is teaching Hindi literature in a college in Uttar Pradesh.

KESARI KUMAR, b. 1909. Has published one volume of verse jointly with Nalin Vilochan Sharma and Narendra Sharma and contributed to various literary journals. Currently Professor of Hindi at Patna University.

KIRTI CHAUDHARI, b. 1935. Has published one volume of poems and contributed to various journals and magazines. Comes from a family of writers. Now lives in Bombay with her husband, Onkarnath Srivastava, also a writer.

KUNWAR NARAYAN, b. 1927. Has published two volumes of poems. Was for some years co-editor of a literary journal published from Lucknow where he also runs an automobile business.

MAITHILI SHARAN GUPTA (1886–1964). Wrote and published continuously for sixty years. Published some forty volumes of verse, including several longer narrative poems. Was awarded honorary D.Litt from Agra University. For many years a nominated member of the Rajya Sabha (upper house of the Indian parliament), from which he retired in 1964. Had been living in his country home in Jhansi until his death.

MAKHANLAL CHATURVEDI, b. 1888. Has published three volumes of poems and one of literary essays. Edited literary and political journals and magazines. Was for many years actively involved in political movements and was imprisoned several times. Was awarded the degree of D.Litt. *honoris causa*. Is Editor, *Karmavir*, Khandwa, Madhya Pradesh.

MALATI PARULKAR, b. 1933. Now Malati Sirsikar by marriage, has published poems and short stories in various literary magazines. Lives in New Delhi.

MALAYAJ [BHARAT VARMA], b. 1940. Has published verse in various journals. Also has translated some poets from the English and has been editorially associated with magazines of new writing.

NALIN VILOCHAN SHARMA (1918–1961). Professor of Hindi at the Patna University up to the time of his death. Published both poems and critical essays in literary journals as well as the joint collection of poems *Naken ke Prapadya* (with Kesari Kumar and Narendra Sharma). Also published a book of literary criticism and one of short stories. Was editor of the literary quarterly *Sahitya*.

NAMVAR SINGH, b. 1927. Took his Ph.D. from Banaras Hindu University. Has taught Hindi literature in Banaras and Saugor. Has published several volumes of literary criticism and contributed to many journals.

NARENDA SHARMA, b. 1913. Has published eight volumes of verse and two of short stories. For some time worked in the office

of the Indian National Congress in Allahabad and edited a
literary journal with Sumitranandan Pant. Has written songs and
dialogues for films. Presently Producer, All India Radio, New
Delhi.

NARESH KUMAR MEHTA, b. 1924. Has published several
volumes of poems, three novels, and two plays. Was for some time
a program assistant in All India Radio and editor of a literary
review now defunct. Lives now in Allahabad.

NAVIN [BALAKRISHNA SHARMA] (1897–1960). Joined the
Indian National Congress in 1920 and was actively involved in
the struggle for Independence; spent several years in prison. For
some years edited the daily *Pratap*, Kanpur. Was a member of
Indian parliament. Published several volumes of verse and one
long narrative poem. Much of his work is still unpublished.

NIRALA [SURYAKANT TRIPATHI] (1898–1961). Published
ten volumes of poems, three novels, and two collections of short
stories. Essays contributed to journals from time to time were
collected in two volumes. Nirala's career was one of continuous
struggle against social tyranny; his later years were embittered by
ill health but his defiant spirit was unsubdued to the last.

PARAMANAND SRIVASTAVA, b. 1935. Has published a volume
of poems and contributed to journals. Is teaching Hindi literature
at St. Andrews College, Gorakhpur.

PRABHAKAR MACHWE, b. 1917. Has published two volumes
of poems, two novels, and two volumes of essays. Contributed to
many journals in Marathi as well as Hindi. Associated with All
India Radio for a few years. Has taught both philosophy and
literature. Was for two years exchange professor at the University
of Wisconsin. Was for a long time Assistant Secretary of the
Sahitya Akademi in Delhi. Now Officer on Special Duty, Union
Public Service Commission, New Delhi.

RAGHUVIR SAHAE, b. 1929. Studied English literature. Was
assistant editor of two literary journals for some years. Worked in
the news division of All India Radio and is now a special corres-
pondent for a Delhi daily. Has published a collection of writings
including poems and short stories. Has contributed to many
journals.

RAMANAND DOSHI, b. 1921. Has published a volume of poems.
Is editing a popular literary monthly from Delhi.

RAMDHARI SINGH DINKAR, b. 1909. Has published six

volumes of poems, a verse play, two volumes of essays, and a survey of the cultural history of India which won a national Academy award. Formerly an officer in the information and publicity department of Bihar, Dinkar was Professor of Hindi at Muzaffarpur College and a member of the Council of States. Is now Vice Chancellor of Bhagalpur University.

RAMSEWAK SRIVASTAVA, b. 1932. Has published a volume of verse. Editor of a literary "little review." Works with the North Eastern Railway in Gorakhpur, Uttar Pradesh. Literary Editor, *Daily Jagram*, Bhopal, Madhya Pradesh.

RAMVILAS SHARMA, b. 1918. Has published a volume of poems and several books of literary criticism. Prominent as a Marxist critic. Took his Ph.D. from Lucknow University and now teaches English literature at Balwant Rajput College, Agra.

RAVINDAR BHRAMAR, b. 1930. Has contributed to journals. Is a lecturer in Hindi at the Aligarh University.

SARVESHWAR DAYAL SAKSENA, b. 1927. Has published a volume of poems and one of prose and verse writings including short stories and a short novel. Was for some years with All India Radio as Assistant Producer. Now on the editorial staff of *Dinman*, Delhi.

SHAMBHUNATH SINGH, b. 1917. Took his Ph.D. in Hindi literature from Banaras Hindu University. Is now teaching Hindi in the Sanskrit University at Banaras. Has published four volumes of poetry and two of literary criticism.

SHAMSHER BAHADUR SINGH, b. 1911. Has published two volumes of poems, one of short stories and sketches, and a book of critical essays about Hindi and Urdu literature. Has written verse in Urdu as well as Hindi. Was for some years editor of a review of new literature. Now lives in Allahabad.

SHRI KANT VARMA, b. 1931. Has published a volume of poems. Edited a literary review from Delhi. Is now on the staff of a news weekly published in Delhi.

SRIKANT JOSHI, b. 1930. Has contributed many poems to prominent Hindi magazines. Has taught Hindi at the college level since 1953. Presently teaches in Post Graduate College, Khandwa, Madhya Pradesh.

SUMITRA NANDAN PANT, b. 1900. Has published over a dozen volumes of poems, a volume of short stories, and two volumes of radio plays. Was for several years Chief Producer, All India Radio, and is now its Literary Adviser. Founded and edited the literary review *Rupabh* (now defunct) with Narendra Sharma as his associate editor.

THAKUR PRASAD SINGH, b. 1924. Currently an officer of the Directorate of Information, Uttar Pradesh. Has been editor of the official magazine *Gramya*. Has published a volume of short stories as well as one of poems.

TRILOCHAN SHASTRI, b. 1917. Has published two volumes of verse and been associated editorily with a poetry magazine. Is a co-editor in the "Dictionary Project" of the Nagari Pracharini Sabha in Banaras.

VISHWANATH, b. 1932. Has contributed verse to various journals. Teaches Hindi at a college in Delhi.

✑§INDEX OF AUTHORS§✑

[125]